Spiritual Shipwreck on the Horizon

Spiritual Shipwreck on the Horizon

Exhorting Christians to Contend for the Faith and Comprehend the Deceitfulness of Sin

R. C. JETTE

RESOURCE *Publications* • Eugene, Oregon

SPIRITUAL SHIPWRECK ON THE HORIZON
Exhorting Christians to Contend for the Faith and Comprehend the Deceitfulness of Sin

Copyright © 2019 R. C. Jette. All rights reserved. Except for brief quotations in critical publications or reviews, no part of this book may be reproduced in any manner without prior written permission from the publisher. Write: Permissions, Wipf and Stock Publishers, 199 W. 8th Ave., Suite 3, Eugene, OR 97401.

Resource Publications
An Imprint of Wipf and Stock Publishers
199 W. 8th Ave., Suite 3
Eugene, OR 97401

www.wipfandstock.com

PAPERBACK ISBN: 978-1-5326-8733-4
HARDCOVER ISBN: 978-1-5326-8734-1
EBOOK ISBN: 978-1-5326-8735-8

Manufactured in the U.S.A.   APRIL 22, 2019

Scripture quotations from The Authorized (King James) Version. Rights in the Authorized Version in the United Kingdom are vested in the Crown. Reproduced by permission of the Crown's patentee, Cambridge University Press.

This book is dedicated to my Lord who gives wisdom and guidance through His Holy Spirit, my husband, my children, my grandchildren, and all who have inspired me in my walk with the Lord.

I want to give thanks to my husband, Paul, and to my daughter, Dawn who have helped me proofread.

A special thanks to Wipf and Stock Publishers who almost seem like family by this time. They have an incredible staff who are professional, patient, and eager to help. Words cannot express my heartfelt thanksgiving to them for publishing, not only this book, but for publishing: *Storms Are Faith's Workout: Preparing Christians for Spiritual Ambush* (2018), *Faith's Journey Confronts Obstacles: Instructing God's Soldiers to Overcome in His Armor* (2019), *Satan's Strategy to Torment Through Physical Ambush: Educating God's Soldiers of Satan's Plot to Shatter Faith Through Sickness and Disease* (forthcoming, 2019), *The Elfdins and the Gold Temple: An Oralee Chronicle* (2018), and *Charlie McGee and the Leprechaun: Life's Curious Twist of Events* (2019)

But I keep under my body, and bring it into subjection: lest that by any means, when I have preached to others, I myself should be a castaway (shipwrecked).

1 Corinthians 9:27.

Contents

Introduction | ix

1. Light | 1
2. Fidelity | 6
3. Workmanship | 12
4. Dominion | 19
5. Occupation | 28
6. Warning | 37
7. Temptation | 43
8. Stumblingblocks | 49
9. Giants | 55
10. Temperance | 62
11. Sentinel | 65
12. Deception | 69
13. Shipwreck | 75

Introduction

This book came about as I pondered my other books concerning faith. I sensed that God was leading me to do another manuscript. When I prayed about it, I saw a ship moving toward the horizon into a tumultuous storm of destruction. In my spirit, I understood that the storm is the deceitfulness of sin that is destroying the faith of many. The Lord was prompting me to do a book that addresses the spiritual shipwreck of faith that is taking place and will accelerate in the last days before Christ returns. He encouraged me with the fact that knowledge will enable us to recognize the deceitfulness of sin and avoid shipwreck. If God's soldiers are prepared, we will not be ambushed by sin's deception.

Prayerfully, those picking up this book have read my other books on faith that are published by Wipf and Stock Publishers and listed in the dedication page. It would be most helpful if my previous books are read, as they are building blocks to strengthen the faith of God's soldiers. Each book reveals greater knowledge and revelation that will prepare us to confront and overcome by faith any obstacle, strategy, or deception that the devil hurls our way. This book will bring forth another truth about faith and will expose why Christians must be aware of the spiritual shipwreck on the horizon that results from the deceitfulness of sin.

At this point, I want to bring forth the intention of this book in transparent terms. It is meant to focus on some signs that could lead to spiritual shipwreck, exhort Christians to contend for the faith, and to expose the deceitfulness of sin. Sin's deception has

Introduction

many of God's soldiers held captive to its deceit. We lack a balanced knowledge of the Scriptures. Through compromise, many of us have become hearers only and not doers of God's word.

Each chapter is intended to unfold some warning that could lead to shipwreck if we don't live its truth. Adherence to living a life that is aware of the deceitfulness of sin must be comprehended by Christians, or we will be brought under its power. I will build on the truths of each chapter in order to construct a foundation that will be solid. Please bear with me in this, as some are so unlearned in Biblical truths, are believing the lies of the devil, are listening to the teachers having itching ears, and are generating compromise. In the last couple of chapters, it will become evident how the deceitfulness of sin has caused the compromise of God's word. Because of the consensus, many Christians are no longer naming sin as sin nor are we standing against its propagation.

We must live a life that earnestly contends for the faith or we will be seduced by the temptations of this world. It is like a drip of water that keeps dripping until it becomes a puddle, then a pool, then a lake, and then an ocean. Leaven starts off microscopic like cancer until it has leavened or corrupted the whole. If we allow a little lethargy, compromise, or seduction in our life, we will be overcome by sin. As we are aware, watchful, and clothed in God's full armor, we will not be shipwrecked no matter how severe the storm of deception.

Christian, you have been struggling with your faith in a calm sea and have no idea of the coming deception that is meant to shipwreck your faith. But the Lord sees your heart and that's why He has directed you to this book. You must realize that my books are not for those desiring teachers having itching ears. They are focused on those who wish to hear, "Well done, thou good and faithful servant . . . enter thou into the joy of thy Lord." Since you have this book in your hands, you are one of those. Don't skip through the pages, but read it through until the end. In being diligent to finish, you will learn how to be aware of the deception of sin, how to contend for the faith, and avoid spiritual shipwreck!

I

Light

> This then is the message which we have heard of him, and declare unto you, that God is light, and in him is no darkness at all. If we say that we have fellowship with him, and walk in darkness, we lie, and do not the truth (1 John 1:5–6).

To COMPREHEND HOW TO avoid the deceitfulness of sin that leads to spiritual shipwreck on the horizon, Christians must understand that God is light and in Him is no darkness at all. In other words, God is only light and there can never be any darkness in Him. In my book about Storms, I explained that whatever God is, He is 100 percent. There is not a hint of the opposite in Him. Since He is love, He is all love. In these verses, He is light and there is no darkness in Him. Therefore, God is wholly light. There is no gray area, shadows, darks, etc. in His light.

What is light? It is the natural agent that stimulates sight and makes things visible. God's light illuminates what was previously not visible to us before. Before we were born again, we walked in spiritual darkness. There was no light of God's truth in our life.

Let's understand more fully the light that God is. According to the Greek, this light is so luminous that no darkness of any kind can penetrate or dull its brightness. It's a light that implies wisdom, holiness, perfection and all that is attributed to good and godliness. It is His light that if we are not born again would extinguish us.

The darkness, or course, is the opposite of light. It's a darkness with no hint of light. Let me explain, when we shut off the lights at night, our vision adjusts to the dark and we can somewhat see. But the darkness in this Scripture refers to a darkness so heavy that we can see nothing. It is like a shroud of density in front of our face that prohibits our seeing even a hint of light.

If Christians are to avoid the spiritual shipwreck on the horizon, we must have a faith that only walks in light. Our God is light, He is perfect, pure, holy, wise, sinless, etc. He is incapable of any darkness of imperfections such as pride, lies, hate, immorality, or any sin. No darkness means that He is void of darkness. Not even a trace of darkness can penetrate His light.

What we must comprehend is that God is to our soul what sunshine is to the world. Without the sun this world would be a very dismal or gloomy place. What a destitute existence we would have with no light and light only perpetual darkness. Without God in our life, our souls are in endless darkness. Our life is shrouded in spiritual apathy.

As we look at what is going on in the world around us, we can understand this truth. Politicians and their followers that are so against God appear to have been given over to a reprobate mind. Let's face it, how can we believe otherwise when they want to murder babies after they are born calling it abortion or women's health care. This is, in fact, sacrificing children to Molech or the devil (Leviticus 20:2-5). I do believe that some are Satan worshippers whose conscience has been seared with a hot iron. Some others have been deceived by the deceitfulness of sin. These are blindly following and need to be warned and delivered from Satan's lies.

With all that is happening, we are definitely in the last days. Scripture makes clear that the last days will be unsafe because men shall love themselves, etc. As we look around, we see self-love has led to the worship of the creation more than the Creator. This fact will become more apparent as we go on. At present, we must comprehend the necessity to walk in His light to comprehend the deceitfulness of sin and to avoid shipwreck.

If we walk in fellowship with God, we have a partnership or communion with Him. The Greek implies a partaking of the Divine nature. In order to be one with God, we must be in agreement with Him (Amos 3:3). Even in the natural, we understand that we cannot spend much time with people who love darkness more than light. That's why God warns us not to be unequally yoked together with unbelievers, because light cannot have communion with darkness (2 Corinthians 6:14).

How can we claim to have fellowship or a companionship of agreement with God who is pure, holy, sinless, light, etc. and walk in darkness? To put it plainly, if we walk in sin, unholiness, lies, jealousy, pride, immorality, and the like, we are not in fellowship with God. In fact, we are in fellowship with Satan who is the god of this world.

> If they speak not according to this word, it is because there is no light in them (Isaiah 8:20).

Unless our life agrees with the word of God, we do not walk in fellowship with Him and we are not walking in His light. If there is unrepented sin in our life, that is darkness and not light. What is emanating from our life? Is light or darkness, good or evil, godly living or ungodly living radiating from us? Is it murmuring and complaining or contentment in the will of God? If we are a light, it is visible to all who watch our life.

I am not claiming that we will be perfect like God, but there should be more light than darkness radiating from us who claim to belong to Jesus. It's as I stated in my book, *Faith's Journey Confront Obstacles: Instructing God's soldiers to Overcome in His Armor*, if we are Christ's no matter how dim our light, it will be seen. A light on a candlestick gives light unto all that are in the house (Matthew 5:15). We are God's lighthouse to others who are sailing in the sea of darkness and heading for destruction.

> Is there no balm in Gilead; is there no physician there? Why then is not the health of the daughter of my people recovered (Jeremiah 8:22)?

The balm that heals God's soldiers is the word of God. The Lord is the Physician. If we remain morally diseased, continue in sin against God, and choose to remain in darkness, it is because we have refused to take the prescription that heals the sin sick soul. It is not merely hearing or reading the word of God, but ingesting it. The word must become part of our very being so that we are spiritually healthy. As a good diet enables us to be physically healthy, the soul's health is dependent on how much of God's word is taken in.

> Thy word is a lamp unto my feet, and a light unto my path (Psalm 119:105).

God's word is the balm or revealer that takes the darkness out of our soul. His word is the light that lightens our path in this life. As His word reveals any deception of sin on the horizon in faith's journey, we see truth and avoid ruin.

Our enabler of light is God's word that makes vision possible. Without light we cannot see in the darkness, we are as blind men. God's word illuminates the sin in our soul. It is like a lighthouse helping the ship to come in safely to harbor.

That which reveals sin, dispels the darkness and enables us to avoid catastrophe. What we have to understand is that faith and light are attributes of God. As we walk in fellowship with Him, we walk in His faith and in His light.

Let's look at this in the natural. God's word is like taking a lamp into a dark place. We hold it up, and it illuminates what is in the darkness. Then we hold it to lighten our path. The light enables us to avoid any obstacles and avoid disaster. However, we must trust that light, have faith in that light, and continue in that light as we travel faith's journey. As we do this, we must trust God that His word will steer us through the deception without shipwreck.

We cannot walk in God's light without a knowledge of His word. As we study God's word, it enables us to rightly divide, understand, and comprehend what it means. It is His word that reveals or shines light on our sin. As we identify the sin and repent of it, the truth or light of His word will expel the darkness or the sin in our lives and enable us to keep walking in His light. As we walk in God's light, we walk according to His word, His will, and His commandments.

Without God's word, there is no light and if no light, there is no fellowship or partnership with God. How can two walk together except they be agreed? No fellowship with God means that instead of light, we walk in darkness. If we walk in darkness, we dwell in sin, poverty, jealousy, pride, sickness, disease, misery, etc. Darkness is all that is contrary to God and is fellowship with Satan.

The more of God's word means the more of God's light. So, if we walk in His light, our fellowship or our partnership is with God where dwells holiness, love, wisdom, health, wealth, happiness, etc. As we partake of His light, we will contend for the faith, comprehend the deceitfulness of sin, and avoid shipwreck!

2

Fidelity

> And he answering said, Thou shalt love the Lord thy God with all thy heart, and with all thy soul, and with all thy strength, and with all thy mind . . . (Luke 10:27).

THE SIGNIFICANCE OF FIDELITY cannot be overstressed. In fact, our devotion to God is the basis or foundation to our overcoming in this life. To love God means to have an esteem and reverence with a deep concern to not offend Him. It means to have a high regard and hold in deep affection. This love is an enormous affection that chooses God above all else.

What this deep affection that we have for God does is to cause us to hate or shun everything that could offend such a holy being. When we offend God we dishonor and displease Him. To love God is to have such reverence, such respect, and such honor for Him that we choose to do nothing contrary to His word or His will. This love triggers us to aim at perfect obedience and to be holy as He is holy (1 Peter 1:15-16).

If we are to walk in God's light, we must love Him with our very being. That means that we are faithful, loyal, obedient, committed, dedicated, constant, etc. to God only. All else in our life is secondary. This is only brought about if we learn to deny self.

Self-love and self-preservation will hinder our love for God. When that happens, self is our top priority and not God. Jesus made it clear that if we lose our life for His sake, we shall find it (Matthew 16:25).

Let's look at our scripture text in Luke. First of all, we must love God with all our heart. Our heart is the center of our feelings or the center of everything that we care about. It is the focus of all that matters to us. If God is not all that matters to us, we will never love Him above all else. Without loving Him completely, we cannot walk in His light. We must learn to walk in the full armor of God and protect our heart from any affection that could mean more than God.

Our soul is our very breath or our very life. In order to love God with all our soul, we must love Him more than our own life. In my book about Storms, I explained about self-love and its hindrance to loving God wholly. It is always self-love that will cause us to love someone, something, etc. more than God. Self is our old nature and it wants to be the god of our life. If it is god of our life, we will indulge in the lust of the flesh, the lust of the eyes, and the pride of life (1 John 2:16). In order to love God above all else, we must deny self daily (Luke 9:23). This means that it is a lifelong endeavor to battle our flesh and allow the Holy Spirit to have His way.

Our mind is our intellectual power, our understanding. It is where we conceive, judge, or reason what media comes into our thinking. The mind is our computer bank where we store all our memory. Whatever our mind conceives, judges, or reasons will yield our intentions, our purposes, our actions, our designs, etc. What we see, what we read, and what we hear are the media that enter our mind. It is the center of our will and however we judge what enters our mind is how we react or respond. Will we choose to believe or not to believe something. That's why if we do not have on the helmet of salvation, wrong thinking can easily sway us contrary to the will of God.

I kept loving God with all our strength as the last one, for it is our ability, our vigor, our energy, etc. It means that we must use all our strength to be stable. We must have toughness of character to withstand whatever the devil tries to attack us with. Let me give an example of what resistance or toughness of character against the devil is like.

> Then was Jesus led up of the Spirit into the wilderness to be tempted of the devil. And when he had fasted forty days and forty nights, he was afterward an hungered. And when the tempter came to him, he said, If thou be the Son of God, command that these stones be made bread. But he answered and said, It is written, Man shall not live by bread alone, but by every word that proceedeth out of the mouth of God. Then the devil taketh him up into the holy city, and setteth him on a pinnacle of the temple, And saith unto him, If thou be the Son of God, cast thyself down: for it is written, He shall give his angels charge concerning thee: and in their hands they shall bear thee up, lest at any time thou dash thy foot against a stone. Jesus said unto him, It is written again, Thou shalt not tempt the Lord thy God. Again, the devil taketh him up into an exceeding high mountain, and sheweth him all the kingdoms of the world, and the glory of them; And saith unto him, All these things will I give thee, if thou wilt fall down and worship me. Then saith Jesus unto him, Get thee hence, Satan: for it is written, Thou shalt worship the Lord thy God, and him only shalt thou serve. Then the devil leaveth him, and, behold, angels came and ministered unto him (Matthew 4:1–11).

Jesus loved God with all His heart, with all His soul, with all His strength, and with all His mind. That's why He was able to confront the devil in the full armor of God. Nothing the devil said got past the armor to sway Jesus away from the truth of God's word. He gave no place for His flesh to get in the way. I mean let's face it, He hadn't eaten or drunk anything for forty days. His flesh was in a weak place, but His Spirit was unmoveable from the truth of God's word. He gave the devil no place to the deceitfulness of sin because He stood firm on the word of God.

Now, let's look at someone else who did not contend for the faith, but gave into the weakness of his flesh. This is an example of self-love and self-preservation.

> And Jacob sod pottage: and Esau came from the field, and he was faint: And Esau said to Jacob, Feed me, I pray thee, with that same red pottage; for I am faint: therefore was his name called Edom. And Jacob said, Sell me this day thy birthright. And Esau said, Behold, I am at the point to die: and what profit shall this birthright do to me? And Jacob said, Swear to me this day; and he sware unto him: and he sold his birthright unto Jacob. Then Jacob gave Esau bread and pottage of lentils; and he did eat and drink, and rose up, and went his way: thus Esau despised his birthright (Genesis 25:29–34).

What we must understand is that Jesus did not love his own life more than God. Esau loved himself and was only concerned about his desire for food. He had the birthright that would have made him in the lineage of Abraham, Isaac, and Esau. But he cared more for his flesh. God's soldiers must see this truth. Too many times there have been remarks about Jacob the supplanter, but little about Esau who was a self-lover and a self-preserver. He loved his life more than God. Esau allowed the deceitfulness of sin to overrule truth. Why else would he ask what good would the birthright do him if he was dead (Genesis 25:32)? The devil had him convinced that he would die, so he listened to the lies, and the deceitfulness of sin induced him to sell his birthright for a fleshly desire.

God did not mean more to Esau than himself, or he would have refused to sell his birthright for the pottage. If he had trusted in the Lord, God would have given him the strength to make it to his mother for bread or had a raven bring him some food. What I am trying to convey is that love of self will interfere with our placing God in His rightful place in our life. As God sent help to Jesus after He withstood the devil and stayed devoted to God (Matthew 4:11), He will do so for us.

Jesus promises as we seek the kingdom of God and His righteousness first, all that we need will be supplied (Matthew 6:33). We must learn not to be concerned about material or physical things. Whatever we need, God will provide. We must deny our flesh and yield to the Spirit as Jesus did. We must not be like Esau and sell our birthright to satisfy a fleshly appetite. Listen up here, our birthright must be everything to us or we will trade it for carnal satisfaction.

As God's soldiers, we must comprehend the importance of loving Him with all our heart, with all our soul, with all our strength, and with all our mind. When we love God with our very life, we will be ready to give up our life for Him. Like I stated in my second book about Faith's Journey, only as we give up the right to our life will we be enabled to endure whatever may come our way.

We must cease to exist. Not literally, but it means that we have chosen to not matter. Our concern is God and His will. It is a departing from self. The "ME" syndrome is the cause of man's Fall, and the cause of man's continuous miseries. Self (our flesh) is contrary to the Spirit and it will always want the opposite of God's will for us.

> But sanctify the Lord God in your hearts . . .
> (1 Peter 3:15).

If we are to depart from self and love God with our whole being, we must sanctify our hearts. Sanctify means separation or set apart. 2 Chronicles 29:19 tells us that the vessels in the Tabernacle were sanctified unto the Lord. In other words, they were set apart for the service of God and were used only for the Him.

1 Peter 3:15 is calling Christians to an inner reverence and commitment to Jesus Christ as one's Lord. We are to give Him His rightful place in our hearts. An inner dedication so devoted to the work of God that we cry "My meat is to do the will of Him that sent me, and to finish His work." (John 4:34). Once we do that, nothing else fulfils us. We are only satisfied in doing His will.

When we sanctify the Lord God in our hearts, we circumcise our hearts. We cut off all the dead skin and all the desires of self or flesh are destroyed. Because our hearts are set apart and used only for God, the so-called pleasures of the world have no appeal to us. For we know that friendship with the world is enmity with God (James 4:4).

Whatever we love most has our heart's affection, our thoughts, our life pursuits, and is what we worship. Who has our fidelity is determined by whether self or God is our greatest love. If it is self, then we are not walking in His light and are out of fellowship with God. If it is God, then we are walking in His light and are in fellowship with Him. Only if God is our God will we fight our flesh, earnestly contend for the faith, comprehend sin's deception, and avoid shipwreck!

3

Workmanship

> For by grace are ye saved through faith; and that not of yourselves: it is the gift of God: Not of works, lest any man should boast. For we are his workmanship, created in Christ Jesus unto good works, which God hath before ordained that we should walk in them (Ephesians 2:8–10).

WORKMANSHIP IS THE SKILL of a workman, or the execution or manner of making any thing. According to the verse in Ephesians, we are God's workmanship. That means that we are not our own to do what we want. We were created in Christ Jesus to do His good works, not what we think is good works.

All of God's works, whatever they may be, are designed to praise and give glory to Him. In other words, all that God does is done so as to point back to Him. He is the One that receives the glory for what has been done.

> I am the Lord: that is my name: and my glory will I not give to another, neither my praise to graven images (Isaiah 42:8).

God is the Creator of all that exists. Only He has the right to boast, to receive honor, fame, or praise on His merit or His own accomplishments. To illuminate this truth, the definition of glorying is the act of exulting, boasting; display of pride. Who of us of our own merit has earned the right to boast about our accomplishments or feats?

> For who maketh thee to differ from another? And what hast thou that thou didst not receive? Now if thou didst receive it, why dost thou glory, as if thou hadst not received it (1 Corinthians 4:7)?

The ability to accomplish whatever we achieve has been given to us by God. He is the One that gives us the gifts, talents, and abilities. For us to boast is to be guilty of pride which goeth before destruction or shipwreck (Proverbs 16:18). God, on the other hand, has not received the ability to perform what He does from anyone. Thus, there is no pride in Him. He is not the workmanship or creation of anyone. We are His creation and all we should be doing is praising Him for all He's done in our life. Our boasting should be in God and not in ourselves. In fact, all we can truly glory about is our infirmities or weaknesses that God turns into strength for His glory (2 Corinthians 11:30; 2 Corinthians 12:10).

Glory is that fame, honor, praise, etc. that is bestowed or attributed to the achievement or work done. With that definition in mind, let's look at God's work and see how it brings forth His glory:

1. God's works of creation proclaim His wisdom and His power.
2. God's works of providence display His goodness.
3. God's works of redemption magnify His love and grace.

The wonder of His works can leave us speechless. When we think of the marvel of redemption, what can we say. To think that God would love us so much that Christ died for us while were in our sinful condition (Romans 5:8). Let's interject here that Christ in order to save us had to die while we were sinners. There is no power over sin until we accept His sacrifice for our sins. That does not infer that we can stay in our sin. It reveals the magnitude of God's grace which divulges that Jesus died to save us from our sins.

When we realize this truth, we cannot but give Him honor, glory, or praise as we behold His amazing grace that made the plan of redemption or salvation possible.

Okay, what does this have to do with Ephesians 2:8-10? It has everything to do with it, for some of us tend to think that we played an important part in our salvation or even our works. Yes, we have a free-will to choose to accept Christ or deny Christ. But we would not have been saved if it had been by our seeking out God to save us.

> As it is written, There is none righteous, no, not one: There is none that understandeth, there is none that seeketh after God. They are all gone out of the way, they are together become unprofitable; there is none that doeth good, no, not one (Romans 3:10-12).

Scripture proves that if God in His love, mercy, and grace did not come after us like a man trying to win his bride, so to speak, we would not be saved. We would still be gone out of the way, not seeking God, not understanding the love of God, and be lost in our trespasses and sins.

> For by grace are ye saved through faith; and that not of yourselves: it is the gift of God: Not of works, lest any man should boast (Ephesians 2:8-9).

God through His grace, which is the free unmerited love and favor of God, grants us mercy, pardon, privilege, favor, etc. It is incredible as we contemplate the whole meaning of grace. Let's comprehend what this is saying to us who have repented of our sins and are trusting in Christ. What blessings have been bestowed upon us? We are recipients of God's love, His grace or favor, His mercy, and His pardon or the privilege of God that we do not deserve.

What have we done that merits such privilege? Our hearts know that we deserve Hell and yet God grants us Heaven. We can claim no merit for our salvation, it is His merit alone. The grace or the influence of God on our heart is the only reason our hearts are renewed. We did nothing to renew our heart.

Even if we abstain from sin, it is still an act of Divine influence. In ourselves, our own merit, we could not save ourselves or keep ourselves from sin. We are not saved by our grace, our merit, etc. Scripture clarifies that we are saved by grace through faith and not of ourselves, it is a gift from God, and not of works lest we should boast.

Some of God's soldiers think that they deserve some honor because of their faith. As I explained in my book, *Faith's Journey Confronts Obstacles*, I deal with the verses in Ephesians chapter two in that book's first chapter. If God did not give us the faith to believe, we would not have faith. Faith is an attribute of God that is fully explained in that same book in chapter eight. This book is meant to build upon my other books not to redo them.

Salvation must be either of grace or works. The two cannot be mixed together any more than oil and water can be mixed together. If it be works in any degree, it is no more part of grace. If it was works in any degree, it would provide occasion for us to boast. For then it would be a debt paid and not a gift bestowed.

The plan of salvation, the Savior who wrought it out for us, the acceptance of His vicarious sacrifice, and the faith whereby we are made partakers of His sacrifice are all the gifts of free and sovereign grace. Salvation's foundation and structure are wholly, totally, and completely of grace.

Let's continue on being His workmanship created in Christ Jesus unto good works, which God hath before ordained that we should walk in them. Here is the difference between our works of righteousness and being His workmanship or His creation in Christ unto good works.

God has given us a new nature and infused into our souls a new and heavenly principle. Under the influence of the Holy Spirit, we move in a new direction. We now affect the things of the Spirit, whereas, we formerly affected the things of the flesh. The new creation is His work, His workmanship, or His creation. When our works are the result of His working in us, it is no longer we that live, but Christ living in us (Galatians 2:20).

Our good works when we behold His salvation, His love, His mercy, His grace, etc. are an obligation. How can we consider what He has done and not feel indebted to Him. What true Christian claiming to be His and to be a recipient of His grace could have no or little desire to please Him?

As God's soldiers desire to please God, good works will be the overflow. What does He desire of us to do when we see our brethren in need? Do we have the means to meet the need? If God is prompting us to be the hands that provide the need, then our gratitude to Him will cause us to willingly supply the need. It is not to be made into a list of what was done or to make people feel indebted to us for being the hands to meet the need. It is obedience to God who will openly bless what we have done in secret. However, if we boast about our giving, we have received our reward.

If we are His creation or His workmanship, our works will show that it is Him working through us and not us. It is by our works that men judge our principles. These are our motives, our cause of action that illuminate what is behind what we do, our objectives, our intentions, etc.

The result of God working though us are that we will:

1. Be the good Samaritan.
2. Walk the extra mile.
3. Meet the needs of the brethren.
4. Be peacemakers.
5. Forgive as we're forgiven.
6. Be a soul winner.
7. Pray for those that persecute us.
8. Live a life of faith in God.
9. Obey Him and His word.
10. Worship only God.
11. Love God with all our heart, soul, mind, and strength.

If we frustrate the grace of God and forbid Him to work those good works through us, we will put a stumblingblock in the way of others and cause them to fall. Our good works are supposed to clear the way for them to Christ. When we become the workmanship of God created in Christ, our works point to Christ and give glory to God.

Our works become good works because they are created in Christ and not in us or ourselves. That means that our works are godly, righteous, merciful. They are Him extending His love, His mercy, His grace, etc. through us. Therefore, even being His workmanship created in Christ unto good works is His gift.

As we can refuse His gift of love, His gift of salvation, etc., we can refuse to be His workmanship of good works. We can refuse to be the vessel that He does good, righteous, merciful, helpful, etc. works through.

If we receive God's gift of grace for salvation, it must include His gift of being His workmanship that allows Him to do good works. He did not offer us the gift of His grace unto salvation and end it there in a place of selfishness. The deceitfulness of sin has too many living in a self-centered salvation that is leading them to shipwreck.

God offered us His salvation that upon our acceptance of it, we live for Him and others. If we were saved for our own satisfaction, then we have no need to be here. However, we are not saved for our gratification, but to be used by the Lord to touch the lives of others in whatever capacity that He has given us the gifts, resources, and talents to do.

The lives that show forth His virtue give glory to Him. The true workmanships or creations of God expose Christ not us. We are not saved by our good works, but we are saved that we may perform good works that glorify God and benefit others.

If we are to avoid the spiritual shipwreck on the horizon, we must realize that we are not here to indulge ourselves. God has saved us that we may deny ourselves and do His will not ours. Too many Christians think that they are saved to spoil themselves. They totally ignore the need in their fellow soldiers. Instead of meeting the need, they offer to pray, or give a handout that has not met the need. How this must grieve the Holy Spirit that pointed out the need to them because they had the means to meet it.

God's workmanships are not here for self-gratification, but to please, to gratify, to delight, and to satisfy Jesus who gave His life to save us. We must not forget His cost, His self-denial, and His suffering for our salvation. What is a little of our time, a little of our resources, etc. to please Him who is our God? When we contemplate all that He has done for us to be His workmanship, we gladly welcome the opportunity to contend for the faith, deny our flesh, obey His prompting, and give Him the glory!

4

Dominion

> And God said, Let us make man in our image, after our likeness: and let them have dominion over the fish of the sea, and over the fowl of the air, and over the cattle, and over ALL THE EARTH, and over every creeping thing that creepeth upon the earth (Genesis 1:26).

THE HEBREW WORD FOR dominion means to tread down, have dominion, prevail against, reign, to rule over. According to Webster's Dictionary dominion means sovereign or supreme authority. This means to have dominion as a king over his kingdom. That was the power or authority that God gave man at creation.

When God created mankind, He gave us the qualities according to His image and likeness. Our first parents possessed the qualities of godliness, righteousness, and intellect. Intellect means the ability to think and to reason. They were free moral agents with the ability to make choices.

Adam and Eve were without sin, sickness, disease, poverty, guilt, shame, etc. Of course, none of these reside in God. Being created in His image and likeness meant none of these attributes resided in them. Now, besides God creating us in His image, He also gave us dominion over all His creation.

The more that we understand the significance of what took place when man fell, the more we can comprehend what was lost. First of all, man switched fathers from God to Satan. When that took place, man died spiritually. At the same time mankind became mortal, the curse of sin and death became his lot. His fallen nature is now created in the image of Satan who is now his god and master. When the devil became his father, God was no longer father.

Yes, God is the Creator of all, but He is not the father of all. Only rejuvenated man is God's child (2 Corinthians 6:17-18). All others are His creation not His children. This was discussed in Faith's Journey. However, it seems to be a truth that many don't understand. What we must comprehend is that when man fell, he not only changed fathers but gave up his right to dominion. The authority that God had given to man was given over to the devil who became the father of unregenerate mankind.

Let's understand that all God gave to mankind, when the Fall took place, transferred from us to Satan. God out of His great love gave man dominion over His creation. Satan out of hate desires dominion for himself. Now, whatever the unregenerate do on this earth is not as the workmanship of Christ, but as the handiwork of Satan. Jesus made clear that those who do not hear His words are of their father the devil and his lusts are what they do (John 8: 44-47).

Mankind no longer has rule or dominion, it was given to the devil in the Garden of Eden. Only God's soldiers who are born again can rule, for we have been adopted by God and are now in fellowship and sonship with God as our Father.

Although that is true, let's understand what is going on in this world as a result of the Fall. Because the devil has dominion or rules the earth, it is full of corruption, wickedness, evil, etc. That's why there is war, crime, hate, terrorism, greed, prejudice, perversion, and malevolent workings of every type.

As long as there is sinful men, evil will exist in every corner of the world. But it doesn't have to rule, have dominion over, or be part of the lives of God's soldiers that confess Jesus as Lord. This chapter will reveal why we are not always living above sin, sickness, disease, poverty, etc. In other words, why are we struggling to live according to all that God gave us at creation?

Why we are lacking in the qualities of God and how we can walk in total dominion will be illuminated in this chapter. We must comprehend that since we have been reinstated to sonship, we have the potential to be like Adam and Eve at creation. The only exception is death which will be the last enemy destroyed (1 Corinthians 15:26).

Jesus' work on the cross enabled those of us who believe to be free from the curse of sin and death. Before we were born again, we were spiritually dead. It was an incredible miracle at salvation that caused the spiritually dead to become spiritually alive. Once we became spiritually alive, we were freed from all the Fall entailed. Sin, sickness, disease, poverty, etc. have no power over us any longer. As was previously stated, it is only death that still has power over us.

The qualities that Adam and Eve possessed are now possible in us who are born again. However, it's not quite that simple. It is not a matter of, "Ah, I'm born again, and I am perfect without sin, sickness, disease, poverty, etc."

> This I say then, Walk in the Spirit, and ye shall not fulfill the lust of the flesh. For the flesh lusteth against the Spirit, and Spirit against the flesh: and these are contrary one to the other: so that ye cannot do the things that ye would (Galatians 5:16–17).

Yes, we are born again and have the potential to live above the curse of sin and death. However, we are now Spirit and flesh. There are now two natures or attributes within us. We are like two persons residing in one body. There is a constant war going on inside with the two natures battling each other (Galatians 5:17). The spirit is trying to gear us toward righteousness, and the flesh is trying to gear us toward unrighteousness.

Our flesh is the fallen Adamic nature created after the likeness of Satan with its desires of the lust of the flesh, the lust of the eyes, and the pride of life. Our Spirit is the new nature created in the likeness of God who is sinless. The spirit person knows to do right, but the evil nature constantly fights to sway us in the opposite direction, the direction that will satisfy or please our fleshly nature instead of God.

Let's look at it this way. It is like we are Dr. Jekyll and Mr. Hyde. Jekyll represents the Spirit and Hyde represents the flesh. Whenever we yield to the peaceful Jekyll or the Spirit, we walk in the fruit of the Spirit. If we yield to the monster Hyde or the flesh, we walk in the works of the flesh. If Christians would get that revelation of the ugliness of the flesh, we would recognize its sinful tendencies and deny it access.

As we yield to the Spirit, we will produce the fruit of the Spirit. If we yield to the flesh, we have the works of the flesh (Galatians 5:18–24). The difference between works and Fruit are that one is works, deeds, labor, or occupation brought forth by our effort. Whereas, the other is not of us. We cannot by our effort produce the fruit of the Spirit, only God can do that. Our flesh is not capable of bearing the fruit of the Spirit. It is produced by the Holy Spirit and Him alone. That's why it is the Fruit of the Spirit and not the fruit of man.

The works of the flesh generate all the lusts that the old nature, the old man enjoy. The main point is that those that do such things will not inherit Heaven or the kingdom of God (Galatians 5:21). According to 1 Corinthians 6:9, the unrighteous, fornicators (sex outside of marriage), idolaters (worship of other gods), adulterers (extra-marital sex), effeminate (unmanly), abuses of themselves with mankind (homosexual), thieves (steal what doesn't belong to us), covetous (desiring what others have), drunkards, revilers (ill-tempered), extortioners (to dissuade, prevent) shall not inherit the kingdom of God. In Revelation 21:8, the fearful, unbelieving, abominable (cursed), murderers, whoremongers (fornicators, adulterers), sorcerers (worship of Satan), idolaters (worship of a god other than the God of the Bible), and all liars shall have their part in the lake which burneth with fire and brimstone.

Fruit that the Holy Spirit produces is love, joy, peace, longsuffering, gentleness, goodness, faith, meekness, temperance of self-control. Against these there is no law.

> For a good tree bringeth not forth corrupt fruit; neither doth a corrupt tree bring forth good fruit. For every tree is known by his own fruit. For of thorns men do not gather figs, nor of a bramble bush gather they grapes (Luke 6:43-44).

We shall be known by what fruit we are bearing. That means that there should be no difficulty differentiating between the good and bad tree. All trees are known by their fruit. Once we understand the works of the flesh and the fruit of the Spirit, we will discern whether it is a good or bad tree.

Let's look at this closer. According to Galatians 5:22-23, the fruit of the Spirit IS. That signifies that the fruit IS singular which means the fruit of the Spirit is one fruit. If we are being led by the Holy Spirit and bearing His fruit, our tree is bearing love, joy, peace, longsuffering, gentleness, goodness, faith, meekness, temperance (self-control). Depending upon where we are in our walk, we may bear more of one than another. However, all components of the fruit will be visible in our life. Our tree is known by our fruit.

If we are not yielding the Spirit's fruit, then we are walking in the flesh and are producing its works. How can we know which we are yielding in our life? Let's look at the difference between fruit and works.

1. Love versus hate, loathing, contempt.
2. Joy versus despair, misery, depression.
3. Peace versus conflict, rage, hostility, agitation, aggravation.
4. Longsuffering, forbearance versus impatience, intolerance.
5. Gentleness versus cruelty, harshness, brutality.
6. Goodness, kindness versus meanness, wickedness, revengeful.
7. Faith, faithfulness versus unfaithfulness, disloyalty, treachery.

8. Meekness versus assertive, overbearing, aggressive.
9. Temperance, self-control or self-discipline versus impulsiveness, no self-control.

Okay, think about the differences between fruit and works. As God's soldiers become aware of the fruit of the Spirit and the antonym (opposite) of the works of the flesh, we can judge whether we are in the spirit or in the flesh. It becomes quite clear if we are Jekyll or Hyde.

When something happens that doesn't bode well with us, how do we respond? Do we respond calmly or in hostility or agitation? The real question here is how do we react in all uncomfortable or irritable situations? We're talking about the times that seem to get under our skin, that trigger us the wrong way, that get to our flesh. Do we yield to the old nature and bring forth the works of the flesh of hate, violence, and lack of self-control? Do we fight our flesh and submit to the Spirit and respond with love, gentleness, and self-control?

Many Christians are responding to life with rage, unfaithfulness, lies, selfish ambition, etc. There's too much vindictiveness, looking to get even. In other words, there is more works of the flesh growing on the trees of Christians than the fruit of the Spirit. We are Spirit and flesh, that is why our tree can bear both. Which one we bear is our choice. If we desire to please God, it will be obvious that we are a good tree. However, if we desire to please self, it will be obvious that we are a bad tree. As we allow the Holy Spirit to have His way in our life, more fruit will be produced. If flesh has its way, we will yield more works of the flesh.

If we walk according to the Spirit, we will not produce the works of the flesh. That which is born of God cannot sin (1John 3:9). That does not mean that we will never sin. As long as we are flesh and Spirit, we will have to battle our flesh. However, the more we yield to the Holy Spirit, the more of His fruit will be seen in our life (tree). The good tree cannot yield bad fruit.

Walking in the flesh will not produce the fruit of the Spirit. The more we react in the flesh, the more works of the flesh will be growing in our life (tree). The bad tree cannot yield good fruit.

What does that mean according to this chapter? It's obvious that we are living below the standards that God gave us. When we were born again, Jesus gave us power and authority over all the power of Satan. We have been given the dominion over sin, sickness, disease, poverty, etc. Yet, because of our yielding to the flesh, the deceitfulness of sin, compromising God's word, we are experiencing the repercussions of the Fall.

It is imperative that we comprehend that the Spirit must have dominion over our flesh. We must deny our flesh and give it no place. Only as we forbid self a place in our life, will we be able to follow Christ (Luke 9:23). It is simply realizing that self doesn't count. If self has no say, we yield to the Spirit and bring forth His fruit.

In the garden before the Fall, Adam had dominion over his human nature. He was without sin, sickness, disease, poverty, etc. Once he fell, he lost dominion over himself and all that God had given to him. Adam chose to disobey God. In doing so, he forfeited all his dominion to the devil. In other words, he gave control of himself to Satan. This must be understood. Adam had dominion over himself and all of God's creation before the Fall. When he fell, Satan now had dominion over him and all God's creation. Before men are born again, Satan can take them captive at his will (2 Timothy 2:26).

> Behold, I give unto you power to tread on serpents and scorpions, and over all the power of the enemy: and nothing shall by any means hurt you (Luke 10:19).

In this Scripture, Jesus is confirming that born again believers have been given back the dominion lost in the garden. Power means authority or dominion. Jesus is saying that He has given us the dominion or authority over all the dominion or authority of Satan. What Adam gave to Satan, Jesus has given it back to God's soldiers.

The treading on serpents or putting them under foot refers to Satan. The Greek for serpent in Strong's Concordance is a snake, an artful malicious person, especially Satan. Scorpions means the sting or strength of the enemy. If we are born again, we have the authority, the right, or the dominion over all that Adam gave to Satan. The only exception is death.

Although the dominion has been given back to us, we have to take it. We have to walk in the dominion. If we are given a new car, but never put the key in the ignition, we will never have the benefit of the new car. It is the same with our enjoying the benefit of dominion over the consequences of the Fall. We have the dominion, like the keys to the car, but we have to use them and walk in that authority. If we allow sin, sickness, disease, etc. to overpower us, we are not walking in that dominion. We have given place to the devil to keep us below our God-given power, authority, or dominion.

> And I will put enmity between thee and the woman, and between thy seed and her seed; it shall bruise thy head, and thou shalt bruise his heel (Genesis 3:15).

> And Jesus came and spake unto them, saying, All power is given unto me in heaven and in earth (Matthew 28:18).

The seed of the woman is Jesus. God promised that the He would bruise the head of the serpent or Satan, and that he would bruise the heel of Jesus. That means that all things of Satan are under the feet of Jesus. After His resurrection or His finished work of redemption, Jesus had power, authority, reign, and dominion in Heaven and on earth.

Satan's demonic dominion was trodden down or trampled under the foot of Jesus. Now, according to Luke 10:19, Jesus gave that dominion back to us. The feet of Jesus are in His body. He is the head of the body, the Church (Colossians 1:18). That means that we as the body of Christ have Satan under our feet.

God's soldiers are freed from the bondage or curse of sin and its affects. But if we walk in the flesh and obey its lusts, we have willingly submitted to the bondage that Christ died to free us from. If we walk in the Spirit, we have the fruit of the Spirit ruling in our life. In this chapter, we must distinguish which of our two natures has dominance. In other words, which one is ruling or has dominion. Is it Hyde/flesh or Jekyll/Spirit?

With spiritual shipwreck on the horizon because of the deceitfulness of sin, we must choose which nature we surrender to. The one yielded to is the one that has dominion. The flesh will lead to spiritual shipwreck because it has no power over self, sin, sickness, disease, poverty, Satan, the earth, etc. The Spirit's power will give authority over self, sin, sickness, disease, poverty, Satan, the earth, etc. Christians that walk in the Spirit comprehend the deceitfulness of sin, take dominion over self, and avoid shipwreck!

5

Occupation

> And now, Lord, behold their threatenings: and grant unto thy servants, that with all boldness they may speak thy word, By stretching forth thine hand to heal; and that signs and wonders may be done by the name of thy holy child Jesus (Acts 4:29–30).

AN OCCUPATION FOR THIS chapter is an activity that we spend time doing. According to our Scripture text, God soldiers should be boldly speaking God's word no matter how much threatenings that we are receiving. Threatenings means to forbid, prevent, or hinder.

> But that it spread no further among the people, let us straitly threaten them, that they speak henceforth to no man in this name (Acts 4:17).

The religious leaders tried to forbid the preaching of the Gospel. The disciples spreading that Jesus was the Messiah had to be prevented. In their self-induced blindness, these Jewish leaders were conspiring against God and not the disciples. They had no intention of entertaining the thought that Christ was their Messiah and they had crucified Him.

When the disciples comprehended what was happening, they prayed and asked God to give them boldness, an assurance, a full persuasion, freedom from doubt to continue preaching. This boldness that they prayed for is a confidence that gives an assurance of mind and a trust that gives courage.

In these last days, God's soldiers must have confidence in God to give them the power that is needed to stand against the lies coming against His word. Evil is being proclaimed as good and good is being proclaimed as evil.

This is seen in our government. Muslims who refuse to uphold our Constitution (the bedrock of our Nation) are in political office. Socialism is being propagated by those who want to take away the voice of "We the People" and make us a country like Venezuela where the people live in a devastating humanitarian crisis. All this is unacceptable to the furtherance of our great Nation that has adhered to the foundational beliefs of our Forefathers. Those who claim to believe in Christ, the Constitution, and the truths of the Bible must awaken to the coming shipwreck, not only to themselves, but, to this Great Nation. Such compromise is causing many to become blind to the warning signs of the dreadful storm created by the deceitfulness of sin, to the voices of Joshua and Caleb proclaiming truth, and to their own conscience.

At this time, I want to interject a story that took place at a Muslim Capital Day in Texas. As the Muslims were celebrating their seventh Muslim Texas Capital Day, Christine Weick interrupted the speaker and proclaimed the Name of the Lord Jesus Christ over the capital of Texas. She stood against Islam and the false prophet Mohammad and stated that Islam will never dominate the United States and by the grace of God it will not dominate Texas.

That's the kind of boldness the disciples were asking for, and that we, as Christ's disciples, must walk in. Jesus made clear that only the truth will set men free from the bondage of sin, the lies of the devil, false teachers, etc. (John 8:32). Once we know truth, we must be like a light on a hill and proclaim it without compromise as that woman did.

> Therefore, my beloved brethren, be ye stedfast, unmoveable, always abounding in the work of the Lord, forasmuch as ye know that your labour is not in vain in the Lord (1 Corinthians 15:58).

In spite of threatenings, persecutions, etc., we, as the disciples, must not allow fear, doubt, any person, or anything hinder us from doing the work of the Lord. We must do God's will no matter what the cost. If we allow self to be instigated by the threats, the truth of God will be hindered. We are not to flee from the enemy, but stand in the faith that assures us that we have the authority. This doesn't mean that we go looking for a contest. But if God says to do something, we stand in His power to accomplish it. As we stand, He will perform the signs, healings, or miracles needed.

It is always a matter of Him increasing and us decreasing (John 3:30). Only as we become less can Christ become more. As self doesn't count or matter, and all that matters is Christ, we place no value on our own life, our desires, our wants, etc.

When our life doesn't matter, and only the will of God matters, there is no threatening, persecution, etc. that will hinder us from doing God's will. In my first book, *Storms Are Faith's Workout*, I explained how self-love and self-preservation cause us to have a lack of faith. That's why God will have no other gods before Him (Deuteronomy 5:7). Self-love and self-preservation make us our own god because "ME" means more to us than God.

> But ye shall receive power, after that the Holy Ghost is come upon you: and ye shall be witnesses unto me both in Jerusalem, and in all Judea, and in Samaria, and unto the uttermost part of the earth (Acts 1:8).

After the Holy Ghost baptism, we are to be witnesses for Jesus. The Greek word for witnesses implies a martyr or one who will die before denying Christ. Thus, as we become less important and Christ becomes all important, our lives, our wants, and our desires don't exist. All we are concerned with is whatever Jesus wants. Our meat becomes that of pleasing God at all costs to self.

The power that we receive after the Holy Spirit has come upon us is supernatural strength, an ability that gives miraculous power to live for Christ and not self. It is the ability to be content in the will of God although it is the opposite of what we may want (Philippians 4:11). It means that when we walk in the Spirit, we are armed and dangerous to the forces of Hell. The devil is a created being and has no power over the God Who created him. Thus, when we stand by faith in His full armor, the devil sees Jesus and not us.

Let's get back to the Scripture text in Acts that states that with all boldness they may speak the word by stretching forth thine hand to heal, and that signs and wonders may be done by the name of thy holy child Jesus.

In order for the power of God to bring forth healing, signs, and wonders through the disciples of Christ, we must trust God with an unmoveable faith. We must comprehend that God cannot work through unbelief or doubt (James 1:5–8). Unbelief stops or hinders Jesus from doing healings, signs, and wonders or mighty works (Matthew 13:58). There is no supernatural power in the flesh. It only takes place by faith in the supernatural. I want to repeat that. There is no supernatural power in the flesh. It only takes place by faith in the supernatural.

Faith reaches the supernatural realm of God, whereas, unbelief or doubt stay in the natural realm of man. In my book, *Faith's Journey Confronts Obstacles*, I gave an example in chapter eight of the mighty works that God can do through us when we believe.

The mighty works that God does are out of the ordinary process of nature. They cannot be performed in the natural. Therefore, we must rise above the natural to the supernatural. Faith does not base itself on the visible but the assurance in God (Hebrews 11:1). Sometimes, it is holding on while our flesh is in agonizing pain (Genesis 32:24–30).

> And these signs shall follow them that believe; In my name shall they cast out devils; they shall speak with new tongues; they shall take up serpents; and if they drink any

deadly thing, it shall not hurt them; they shall lay hands on the sick and they shall recover (Mark 16:17–18).

Name in the Greek implies that the use of that Name carries the authority and the character of the person of Jesus Christ. This is saying that Christ has given to God's soldiers the power of attorney to use His name. As Jesus performed supernatural signs or miracles, we, through His name, are supposed to have such signs following us. Signs should accompany or be present as the result of them that believe.

Those that believe in the name of Jesus and have faith in the authority and character of Jesus should have the power of God, supernatural signs, healings, miracles accompanying or following that faith. Signs should be present in the life of God's soldiers that believe in Jesus. However, if our faith is that of James chapter one that hesitates, doubts, and wavers, nothing will accompany our wavering faith.

God made clear that anyone with a vacillating conviction will not receive from the Lord. Our faith must be one of boldness and not fear to come against those who would compromise God's truth. We must have unwavering confidence in who God is and in His ability to do whatever He says. This was the kind of faith the disciples possessed when they asked for confidence to speak God's word. They knew that God will not work in unbelief. Only steadfast faith in God's word would enable Him to stretch forth His hand to heal and perform signs and wonders.

Let's understand something here, it is not us who do the actual signs, wonders, and healings. They are performed by Jesus when we are confident or have unwavering faith in Him to do what we have asked. We cannot do the impossible, but God can (Luke 1:37). We cannot speak the worlds into existence, but God did (Genesis 1). He is the same yesterday, today, and forever (Hebrews 13:8). Whatever impossibility that He did yesterday, He can do today and forever. When we believe, He reciprocates that faith.

What we must comprehend is that the supernatural is not natural to us, for we are fleshly and of the natural realm. God is Spirit and of the supernatural realm. The supernatural is the natural to God. He has no limits as we do. He is everywhere present at all times. We can only be in one place at a time. God knows all things past, present, and future. We are limited in what we know. We do not know all things and that is why we must trust Him when we don't understand something that is happening.

God cannot doubt, hesitate, for God is faith. I brought this truth forth in my book , *Faith's Journey Confronts Obstacles*. It was God's faith that took nothing and made all things visible and invisible. In other words, God made all things from what did not exist before His faith brought it into existence (Hebrews 11:3). Because God knows who He is, that He is capable of doing all things, He has no unbelief, and He does them.

The power of God, healings, signs, and wonders are not part of the natural realm, the place of doubts, hesitations, etc. Our eyes of faith must look to the supernatural, that which our natural eyes cannot see.

By this time, God's soldiers are thinking that if these supernatural signs should be present in our lives, where are they? What's going on? The question that we must ask is why didn't Jesus do many mighty works? Scripture makes clear that it is from their unbelief (Matthew 13:58). To have unbelief means to disbelieve or doubt.

Whenever there is disbelief, there is faithlessness and disobedience to God's word. We hesitate, doubt, question, waver, procrastinate, fear, etc. Because of our unbelief or doubt our disobedience means there will be a lack of the power of God, supernatural healings, signs, and wonders in our life. If the just shall live by faith (Hebrews 10:38), we are disobedient to God's word when we doubt, question, fear, or procrastinate. In other words, we lack faith in God's ability to perform what He promised.

God does not say in Mark chapter sixteen that these signs might, maybe once in a while, or sporadically be present. No, He emphatically states that they will be present in the life of those that believe in His name. When we entrust our spiritual well-being to Christ, have confidence in Christ's ability to perform His word, we shall experience the power of God with these signs present in our lives.

The disciples knew Jesus could and would perform His word. That is why despite the religious leaders forbidding them to speak the word of God, they asked for boldness or the confidence needed to withstand the persecution and preach the gospel. They knew that as they preached the gospel in faith that Jesus would follow it with the signs and wonders that His word proclaims.

When God's soldiers stand firm, believe God above all else, and do not look or listen in the natural realm of man's knowledge, wisdom, medicine, science, psychology, etc. He will perform those supernatural healings, signs, and wonders through us.

> Verily, verily, I say unto you, he that believeth on me, the works that I do shall he do also; and greater works than these shall he do; because I go unto my father (John 14:12).

Works in the Greek means occupation, deed, or labor. Christ's works or His occupation was the power of God in His life doing healings, signs, and wonders. The power of God in Him enabled Him to rule self. He gave no place to any sin. God's power working in us will give us the power over self and sin. As we rule self or the flesh, we are enabled by faith to yield to God. When the Spirit rules and not the flesh, God's power with healings, signs, and wonders will follow our life.

Faith is not about how hard we can believe. It is how much we know about God that strengthens faith or that encourages faith. We gain faith through hearing or understanding the word of God (Romans 10:17).

Thus, the longer we walk with the Lord and get to know Him, by reading, hearing, studying, learning, and understanding His word, the more we love and trust Him. The greater the degree of our love and trust, the greater or stronger becomes our faith in Him. If we have little word, we have little love, little knowledge and that yields weak faith. If we have more word, we have more love, more knowledge and that yields strong faith.

Our faith must be strengthened to stand up against the wickedness that is rampant in our society today. Scripture makes clear that evil is going to worsen (2 Timothy 3), and that's why we must have courage to stand against it as that woman in Texas did. As God gave the disciples boldness to come against the religious leaders, He will give us the power to take authority over the devil's lies. However, we must not join the crowd that is compromising God's word and heading for spiritual shipwreck.

The less we know about God, the more we walk in the natural realm that is void of His power with healings, signs, and wonders. This is where compromise is exchanged for the truth of God's word. We end up with the wrong understanding of God and listen to those that a loving God won't send anyone to Hell. Jesus taught us to love our enemies, so we are not to come against them.

God will not send anyone to Hell, we choose to go there. When we refuse to accept His sacrifice on the cross, refuse to live godly, refuse to obey His word, etc., we have chosen Hell. Revelation 21:7 makes clear that only we that overcome (conquer, defeat, surmount) shall inherit all things. God only gives eternal life to us that do things His way and not ours.

When we refuse to come against the lies that Satan is propagating, we have chosen to deny Christ and His truth. Jesus did not stand idly by as the religious leaders taught the people wrong doctrine or turned God's house into a house of merchandise (Matthew 23:15; John 2:13-16). The more we know about God, we will, by faith, be enabled to rise above the natural realm into the supernatural realm where the power of God will strengthen us to name sin as sin. That's the place where we stand in the full armor of God and the truth of God's word overrules compromise, etc.

We cannot have the supernatural in our life if we believe the natural. In my book, *Satan's Strategy to Torment Through Physical Ambush*, I mentioned that the doctors said that there was no cure for ulcerative colitis and that I would have to live with it.

The choice to believe the doctors or God's word was mine. The Holy Spirit had impressed me that He created my body to heal itself. I will not go into detail about what is in the other book, but I believed God. I had to get out of the natural realm of man's knowledge, science, medicine, etc. and rise by faith into the supernatural realm of healings, miracles, etc.

When Jesus walked this earth, He knew that what God says, He can and will do. His Faith was confident, He had boldness to speak the word tenaciously. Because Christ's faith was one of confidence in God's ability, the power of God with healings, signs, and wonders were present in His life. There was no compromising the truth of Scripture with Jesus, and He expects the same from us. Jesus named sin and that's what God's soldiers must do. If we don't name sin as sin, we will be denying the truth of God's word. This surrendering will be made more evident as we go along.

If God's soldiers are doing, living, and believing God's word, the power of God, healings, signs, and wonders will be common place in our lives as they were with Jesus and the early Church. It is not this author stating this, but Jesus promised it in John 14:12.

Once we have unwavering confidence in God, His word, and His ability to perform His word, the signs that are promised will follow His word spoken with bold faith. As we speak the word of God with the boldness of Christ, stand against the evil of today, and expect the miracles to accompany it, they will be present (Hebrews 11:6).

Christians must realize that when we waver in our faith, we are heading toward the horizon and shipwreck. If we stop fighting our flesh, and start to lean more on the natural realm, spiritual shipwreck is inevitable. As we understand the need to lean more on the supernatural, our occupation will be that of Jesus who never faltered in His faith. The power of God flowed through Him as He stood against the lies of His day, contended for the faith, and named sin as sin. Only as we follow Him in the supernatural realm, will we walk in the power of God, contend for the faith, and name sin as sin!

6

Warning

> Wherefore let him that thinketh he standeth take heed lest he fall (1 Corinthians 10:12).

THE APOSTLE PAUL GIVES a warning to take heed. In other words, we are to beware of thinking we are standing and become prideful. Before continuing, I will give a story about a minister from England who taught on this Scripture at a teaching one night in Connecticut. He was staying at a minister's house here in the states. Anyway, the preacher had a jacuzzi in his bathroom and the English preacher was patting himself on the back on how much he deserved to enjoy the jacuzzi. As he was being prideful, he heard, "Wherefore let him that thinketh he standeth take heed lest he fall." He was tired, sore, got into the jacuzzi, and continued to boast about how he earned this comfort. Anyway, he finally got out of the tub and fell down the step. If he thought he needed the jacuzzi before, he really needed it now. That night at the teaching, he was quite uncomfortable. He had an amazing personality and said that what he was going to teach on, the Lord had completely changed his mind.

He taught about pride and how we can begin to think that it is us doing what we do and forget that whatever God's soldiers do is through the power of the Holy Spirit. Sometimes, we can become so proud of our work for the Lord that we can think we deserve His blessings. He laughed and said God knows how to keep us humbled if we get boastful. Reverend Doctor Ivor Nicklin was an incredible minister of the Lord. Anytime that he was in the states, we tried to make it a point to go where he usually ministered until we moved from New England.

Our Scripture texts says, "Let him that thinketh he standeth take heed lest he fall." To think is to suppose, to form an opinion which may be either right or wrong. This means that thinking will not keep us on our guard against falling. The fall is to descend, to fall down from, a falling into temptation, or a falling under judgment. Genesis chapter three describes that human temptation comes, not from God, but from Satan. Adam and Eve were forced to decide for or against God.

In Job chapter one, Satan appears as the tempter. We see the temptation here is allowed by God as a test. Job meets the test because, even in incomprehensible suffering, he is ready to count on God and commit himself to Him. However, we did see that when Job was attacked physically, he began to accuse God of being unjust. We also saw that Job had a wrong belief of God which contributed to his incorrect assessment. Once God confronted him, Job saw the error of his belief and repented. I will not elaborate upon Job here as this is discussed in my first book, *Storms Are Faith's Workout*, and then at length in my book, *Satan's Strategy to Torment Through Physical Ambush*.

We can think that we are standing. As a matter of fact, we can stand in right relation with God, and yet, begin to waver in our faith and fall into unbelief. When this happens, we will bring down Divine discipline upon ourselves. God's soldiers may have His favor so far as concerns outward entitlements, and yet perish as many of the Jews did in the Wilderness. Therefore, if we think that we are standing whether our apprehension is true of false, we had better use all means and caution to not fall into temptation and end up in spiritual shipwreck.

WARNING

Sometimes the term "temptation" signifies motions made by the lusts and unrenewed part of our own souls. That means the part which God has not been allowed to renew or we are too young in the Lord for it to be renewed yet. For instance, we can find ourselves dealing with things that we thought were long gone. This can take us off guard to find that we are facing a temptation to something that we thought had been done away with.

The truth is that God allowed a band-aid to be put over that part of our life until we were mature enough in Him to handle it. Sometimes, we have had such hurt that until we can truly deal with forgiveness, it is somewhat hidden. Then all of a sudden, the band-aid is removed, and we feel the hate, the anger, the hurt, etc. at what was done to us. It is dross that has been brought up to the surface to once and for all be dealt with. However, if we fail to deal with it according to God's word, we will have rejected His grace that is promised in time of need (Hebrews 4:16). Christians must understand that when the band-aid is removed, it is because the Lord wants us to be healed from the wound. In my first book about storms, I revealed some things about forgiveness and the release that is experienced when it is truly done from the heart.

Paul was warning all that no matter how we stand, we had better be in watching and prayer, lest we fall into temptation. It is a warning to always be in self-evaluation of our motives, our thoughts, etc.

The Lord impressed my heart as a young Christian that the heart is deceitful above all else and desperately wicked (Jeremiah 17:9). That means if we yield to our old nature, it is essentially depraved. If we are not transformed in our minds, the deceitfulness of sin will deceive us into believing that we are justified in not forgiving the person for what they did. We will be deceived into believing that we had no choice but to tell that lie. We will be deceived into believing that we cannot overcome that vice. After all, we are only human. We're not God like Jesus is. He overcame because He is God, but we are fallen mankind.

All are lies from the devil who tempted Eve into disbelieving the word of God. Scriptures make plain that we are only forgiven as we forgive others (Luke 11:4). Revelation 21:8 makes clear that all liars shall have their part in the lake which burneth with fire and brimstone. When Jesus became man, He made Himself of no reputation (Philippians 2:7). In other words, He emptied Himself, gave up His divine privileges, and was here as a man. Jesus was capable of being tempted just as we are and that's why He can understand our temptations and give us power over them (Hebrews 4:15).

What we must comprehend is that God's soldiers who confidently stand are those of us who have the fullest conviction that our heart is right with God and our mind is right in the truth. We are fully clothed in the full armor of God and stand against the wiles of the devil. It is imperative that we always take heed or beware that we are fully armored at all times. Neglecting any part of the armor could cause us to fall into unbelief and from the state of holiness in which the grace of God has placed us. For instance, if we are standing in pride and not in humility, we will fall. Christians can sometimes become prideful of their work for the Lord and begin to think that they deserve to be pampered. However, it is imperative that we realize that no matter what we do for the Lord, we are unprofitable servants doing that which is our duty to do (Luke 17:10). As we comprehend that truth, we are kept in a proper frame of mind.

You see we are in a continuous state of probation in this life and everything could change just like that. We can stand one moment and then fall the next. Our standing is contingent upon our faith in God, our trusting in His love, and loving Him absolutely. That depends upon our watching unto prayer and continuing to possess faith. My first book revealed how the Israelites had incredible faith after crossing the Red Sea and when times became hard, they fell into unbelief. That's why no matter how much faith we may have today, if we become a hearer only and cease to do the word, we will fall into sin. When this happens, our understanding becomes darkened and our heart becomes hardened like flint.

WARNING

> For our light affliction, which is but for a moment, worketh for us a far more exceeding and eternal weight of glory; while we look not at the things which are seen, but at the things which are not seen: for the things which are seen are temporal; but the things which are not seen are eternal (2 Corinthians 4:17-18).

Paul was telling the Corinthians that their trials were trivial in comparison to those suffered by the Israelites and might have been easily forborne and conquered. They had the Holy Spirit living in them to help, whereas, the Israelites did not.

Now, look at God's soldiers today who not only have the Holy Spirit living in them, but have access to the Scriptures which includes the wilderness example. The Israelites only had the ten commandments to rely upon. We live in the Age of Grace; they lived in the Age of the Law. Because we are under grace, sin does not have dominion over us as it did under the law (Romans 6:14).

Let me explain this. Before grace, sin reigned over us. Christ's atonement on the cross dethroned Satan and his power of sin, sickness, disease, etc. Now, because of Jesus, God's soldiers have power over sin. It is our choice whether it rules in our life or not (Romans 6:12). However, it is a constant battle of the flesh against the spirit (Galatians 5:17). We are not set free from sin's temptations when we are born again, but we are given the power over it through grace. If we give into sin's desire, it will overpower us. But it cannot rule over us unless we allow it to. Whereas, under the law there was no power over sin (Romans 6:14).

That's why Paul gave the warning against being prideful in thinking that we stand on our own. We must walk circumspectly at all times and be mindful that whenever we turn from our steadfastness, we will fall into sin.

The reason for us to be mindful of taking heed is that this book is concerned with the spiritual shipwreck on the horizon and the necessity to comprehend the deceitfulness of sin. I believe that we are on the horizon of the latter days, the deceitfulness of sin is a widespread storm, and many have become shipwrecked. They have left the faith of the Bible and are following after fables and whatever else pleases their fleshly appetites.

But to God's soldiers who are fighting the good fight of faith, be of good cheer for Jesus has overcome the world (John 16:33). Through the power of the Holy Spirit, we will comprehend sin's deception, contend for the faith, and overcome as He did!

7

Temptation

> There hath no temptation taken you but such as is common to man: but God is faithful, who will not suffer you to be tempted above that ye are able; but will with the temptation also make a way of escape, that ye may be able to bear it (1 Corinthians 10:13).

TEMPTATION IN THE GREEK means a putting to proof (by experiment of good or of evil; solicitation, entice). An understanding of this Scripture will determine victory or defeat during the time of temptation. The devil is the tempter (Matthew 4:3 11) and he is relentless in his plan of seduction to lure us away from the truth of the Scriptures. He is so bold that he tried to tempt Jesus. However, Christ was not only knowledgeable in the word, but He knew how to rightly divide it. Jesus stayed clothed in the full armor of God and was proficient in the sword of the Spirit which is the word of God. Christians must understand that we don't have to fall prey to temptation. If we are enticed by the deceitfulness of sin, we could find ourselves shipwrecked. Let's look at the Scripture reference above and see its main points.

1. What is true about every temptation we face?
    a. They are common to all men.

> b. There is no new type of temptation.
>
> c. None of us have a monopoly on any certain temptation.
>
> d. We are not the first to be tempted with the enticement.

2. Who can give us victory when we are tempted?

    a. It is God who is faithful to make a way.

3. Does He promise to remove the temptation?

    a. Of course not.

    b. Too many pray, "God, please take away this temptation."

    c. "You promised that I won't be tempted more than I am able."

4. What does God actually promise to do?

    a. He promises to make a way of escape or an escape route.

    b. He will make a way out that enables us to bear the temptation and not be shipwrecked by it.

As we travel along faith's journey, we will face many temptations with numerous crossroads and intersections. Satan is the tempter who is always trying to get us to make a wrong turn. In other words, he is continuously trying to seduce, entice, or lure us into sin. Now, we know that Satan is the tempter, but what is the major source of temptation? James 1:13–14 makes clear that our own lusts are how we give into temptation.

At this time, I will interject a story. A man in the Church had lost his mother and he was overcome with grief. He was angry at his wife because her mother was older than his mother and was still alive and healthy. Anyway, he began to spend time with another woman at work. When they were in a adulteress situation, I confronted him. He told me that it was God who sent her to him to help him get over his mother's death like Rebekah helped Isaac over the loss of his mother. Needless to say, the devil had deceived him and seduced him with lies. I had to give him the truth of the Scriptures that God doesn't tempt anyone. When His word says that no adulterer will inherit the Kingdom of God (1 Corinthians 6:9), He means just that. I told him that he was a selfish man to be jealous that his wife's mother was still alive. Anyway, to make a long story short, he refused to hear truth of the Scriptures, divorced his wife, and about a year later died in an accident.

The point of this is that we are drawn away into sin by our own lusts. Whenever we are tempted and yield to the lusts of the flesh, the lusts of the eyes, and the pride of life, we fall prey to the enemy. If we do well, sin will desire us, but we will rule over it. If we don't do well, sin is lying at the door, and it will overcome us (Genesis 4:7).

Any time we say, "God, I can't take this anymore," or "this is more than I am able to bear," we have called God a liar. It is doing what the devil said Job would do. We are literally cursing God to His face. Listen to me, God says that our trial is common to all men, and that He has promised a way of escape or a way to endure.

Our way of escape or way to endure is His love and His word. It is hanging on and not letting go. How do you think the Christians in my book on faith, *Satan's Strategy to Torment Through Physical Ambush: Educating God's Soldiers of Satan's Plot to Shatter Faith Through Sickness and Disease* were enabled to endure such persecution? It was not their own strength. We can only endure as we trust in the love of God and loving Him with our very life. Those early Christians knew, according to His word, that what they were about to endure was for a moment. But when it was over, they would be in glory with their Savior (2 Corinthians 4:17).

Let's understand that a temptation cannot overtake us without our choice. Every temptation comes before the moment of decision. What does that mean? If we are driving down the road and we come to an intersection, we choose what direction to take. On faith's journey, when we come to a crossroad of temptation or the way out, the Holy Spirit will prompt our heart which road to take. All born again believers are promised that the Holy Spirit will guide us into all truth (John 16:13). That means that no matter the temptation, the Holy Spirit will cause a hesitation through the word of God. None of us claiming to be a Christian goes right into a temptation unless we have ignored the warning, listened to the deceitfulness of sin, and yielded to the desire of our flesh.

Let me give some examples of a crossroad by listing some temptations and the way of escape:

1. *Temptation*: Evil thoughts.
   Escape Direction: Let the words of my mouth, and the meditation of my heart, be acceptable in thy sight, O Lord, my strength, and my redeemer (Psalm 19:14).

2. *Temptation*: Too tired to go to Church.
   Escape Direction: Not forsaking the assembling of ourselves together, as the manner of some is; but exhorting one another: and so much the more, as ye see the day approaching (Hebrews 10:25).

3. *Temptation*: To tell a lie or sow discord among the brethren.
   Escape Direction: The Lord hates a lying tongue and sowing discord among the brethren is an abomination to the Lord (Proverbs 6:16–19).

4. *Temptation*: Date or go into business with a non-believer.
   Escape Direction: Be ye not unequally yoked together with unbelievers (2 Corinthians 6:14–18).

5. *Temptation*: Murmuring and complaining.
   Escape Direction: Do all things without murmurings and disputings (Philippians 2:14).

Satan has tempted us with the temptation. The Holy Spirit has quickened with the way of escape. That's when the devil will further tempt us with lies about the Lord. He will imply that we are too weak to overcome this obstacle. However, the Lord promises that we can do all things through Christ which strengtheneth us

(Philippians 4:13). He will insinuate that God expects too much from us. Yet God promises that we are never tempted with more than what we can handle (1 Corinthians 10:13).

God will not remove the temptation. It is up to us to make the right decision. It is time for God's soldiers to quit blaming Him for the messes in our life. We must choose to avoid whatever could tempt us into sin. It is imperative that we realize that there are certain situations where we could give place to the devil. For instance, if we had a problem with pornography, why are we at the beach, etc.? If we had overcome alcoholism, why are we at that drunken party? If we had a problem with drugs, why are we around those who are addicted? Some of us have been completely delivered, but others are still battling the temptation to go back. Wisdom is justified of her children (Luke 7:35). God will never direct us to be where temptation could shipwreck us.

Let me make something clear here. All temptations are like intersections. We are the ones that decide which direction we take. Do you remember when vehicles didn't have power steering? Well, when we are at the moment of decision, we must turn ourselves like we did the vehicle in the direction to go. Sometimes turning the truck was quite a challenge. That is the way it is at times for us. Fighting our flesh to contend for the faith can be quite exhausting, but it must be done if we are going to overcome this life.

We cannot stay forever at an intersection or crossroad. The tempter has tempted us, and the Holy Spirit has given us the word that is our escape route. Now, we are at the moment of decision. The devil cannot make us do anything against our will, and the Holy Spirit will not make us do anything against our will. It is our decision which way we go. Whether we love God more than self will determine which voice we listen to, and what direction we take.

As we travel faith's journey, it is not a matter of all roads meet in the end. There is only one way to get to where we are heading. The straight and narrow way that leads to life will be extremely difficult on our flesh. Whereas, the wide and broad way that leads to destruction is extremely agreeable on our flesh with its lusts and appetites (Matthew 7:13–14). One road is living a life of self-denial of all that is unrighteous and the other road is a life of self-indulgence of all that is unrighteous.

If we are driving someplace and we don't follow the directions, we will not end up at our destination. That same principle must be followed at the time of temptation. Only as we follow the straight and narrow that constricts our flesh will we end up in Heaven. Following the broad and wide that indulges our flesh will lead us to Hell. There is no middle road. It is either one or the other. Flesh will choose the broad and wide that leads to destruction. Spirit will choose the straight and narrow that leads to life.

All good drivers have Insurance. Ours includes: God's full armor, prayer, knowing and heeding God's word, coming boldly before God for the promise of help, yielding to God while working against the devil, and having faith (Ephesians 6:10-18; Matthew 6:9,13; Psalms 119:9,11; Hebrews 4:16; James 4:7; 1John 5:4). This reveals that it takes an effort on our part. We must initiate the resistance against the temptation. If we crucify our flesh and its lusts, God will help us to succeed. He cannot resist for us. It is our free will that decides what we do. We can be assured that if we fight and wrestle our fleshly desires and yield to the Holy Spirit, He will show the way of escape that disables the deceitfulness of sin!

8

Stumblingblocks

And the word of the Lord came unto me, saying, Son of man, these men have set up their idols in their heart, and put the stumblingblock of their iniquity before their face: should I be enquired of at all by them? Therefore speak unto them, and say unto them, Thus saith the Lord God; Every man of the house of Israel that setteth up his idols in his heart, and putteth the stumblingblock of his iniquity before his face, and cometh to the prophet; I the Lord will answer him that cometh according to the multitude of his idols. That I may take the house of Israel in their own heart, because they are all estranged from me through their idols. Therefore say unto the house of Israel, Thus saith the Lord God; REPENT, and turn yourselves from your idols; and turn away your faces from all your abominations (Ezekiel 14:2-6).

WHAT EXACTLY IS A stumblingblock? It is something that causes an impediment to belief or understanding. Anything that is an obstacle, barrier, snag, hitch, weakness, defect, etc. to our faith is a stumblingblock that must be removed or overcome.

The Scriptures in Ezekiel inform us that the stumblingblocks were caused because of idols that are set up in our heart. This means that the hindrances are self-induced. Whether the devil is involved or not is not the point. It is God's soldiers that have allowed iniquity in our life and it has caused us to stumble.

Whenever we become a hearer only of God's word and do not adhere to obeying it, we have opened the door for an idol to be set up in our heart. How is that? Because our idol starts with self that doesn't believe that it must do what the Scriptures say. We cannot blame anyone if we become deceived. We heard the word, decided not to obey, and became deceived by our own selves. The choice to believe that it didn't refer to us or it wasn't important for us to obey was ours.

> Thou shalt have no other gods before me (Exodus 20:3).

God will not permit any rival with Him. God's soldiers are to worship Him and only Him. That means that no person, place, thing, etc. can have preeminence in our heart that could interfere with our loving the Lord with all our heart, with all our soul, and with all our mind (Matthew 22:37). This is not heartlessness on God's part. He knows that if we are not totally dedicated to Him, we will place other gods first, and we will not overcome in this life.

Although this was talked about in Chapter two, I felt that it must be reiterated. It is essential that we understand the importance of loving God above all else. As we love God with all our heart, there isn't anything that can compare to our devotion to Him. We are willing to give up all for Him in order to please and glorify Him in all things. God becomes our greatest desire, the center of all our affections, our whole life becomes His to direct. However, if we don't understand God's love for us, we will not love Him the way that is necessary to overcome. This is revealed in my book, *Storms Are Faith's Workout*. Our love for God must be one of self-denial where only what He wills is our desire.

When we love God with all our soul, it means with our very breath. This love causes us to love God more than our life. The martyrs mentioned in my book, *Satan's Strategy to Torment Through Physical Ambush* definitely loved God more than their own life. If they hadn't, they could not have suffered such persecution for the Name of Jesus. In my first book about Storms, I explained self-love. When self is first, we will never be willing to give our life for Christ.

To love God with all our mind is to love Him with all our intellectual power or our understanding. Our mind is where we conceive, judge, or reason which yields our intentions, our principles, and our plans. Everything that enters our mind must be conceived, evaluated, and analyzed. How it is analyzed determines our actions and our beliefs. Whatever we do is the result of what has been through our thought process. Our mind is the center of our will, and our will is where we choose to believe God or to not believe God.

What is happening is that many of us are setting up idols in our hearts that have become stumblingblocks. This has happened because we ignored the full armor of God and permitted the lies of the devil to cause us to doubt the word of God. If we neglected the helmet of salvation, the girdle of truth would have shone light on the dark lie. Then the shield of faith and the sword of the Spirit which is the word of God would have cut to pieces the lies of the enemy.

> Now Sarai Abram's wife bare him no children: and she had an handmaid, an Egyptian, whose name was Hagar. And Sarai said unto Abram, Behold now, the Lord hath restrained me from bearing: I pray thee, go in unto my maid; it may be that I may obtain children by her. And Abram hearkened to the voice of Sarai (Genesis 16:1–2).

This story is an excellent example of how an idol in the heart can become a stumblingblock. Abraham and Sarah desperately wanted a child. When God gives us a promise, we can become weary in waiting for it to come to pass (Galatians 6:9). That is a dangerous place for us to be. God never puts a time frame from the seed of the promise until it is harvested. Galatians 6:9 makes obvious that we can become fatigued in our waiting or our well-doing. During the time of the wait, we can start to lean on our own understanding.

Sarah believing that there was no way for her to give birth at her age decided to help God out. Abraham knew that God had promised him an heir that would come forth out of his own bowels, so he agrees with Sarah that Hagar must be the way for it to be accomplished. Their desire for the heir was the idol in their heart that became the stumblingblock which caused them to lose faith in God and take things into their own hands. Of course, that stumblingblock is threatening Israel and the whole world today with Ishmael (Islam). As Ishmael hated Isaac the child of faith, Muslims hate Isaac's progeny (Jews) and Christians today.

How many of God's soldiers today have been given a promise, become weary in the wait or well-doing, and decide how the promise will be accomplished. We start to rationalize what God must have meant until our logic has overruled faith. It is no longer faith that God can do the impossible (Luke 1:37), but how can we cause the promise to happen.

If we want something and God is taking too long to bring it about, we yield to our flesh that is tired of waiting. When we decide that enough is enough, the promise becomes an idol in our heart. Once it is set up as an idol in our heart, it becomes a stumblingblock or an impediment to faith. The fact is that as Ishmael was the child of the flesh, whatever we bring forth in the flesh will have consequences.

> Wherefore seeing we also are compassed about with so great a cloud of witness, let us lay aside every weight, and the sin which doth so easily beset us, and let us run with patience the race that is set before us (Hebrews 12:1).

The weights are hindrances or stumblingblocks that obstruct the progress of our journey of faith. As we saw, the stumblingblock in Abraham and Sarah was the idol in their hearts of desiring an heir. Whatever we desire in our flesh becomes an idol in our heart and becomes the stumblingblock that hinders us from living by faith. Is it the desire for a better job? Is it the desire for a husband or a wife? Is it the desire to have children? Is it the desire for a better house? All of these desires may be a promise from the Lord that is taking too long for fruition. Our flesh has convinced us that perhaps He meant for it to be this way, etc.

When this happens, we have a struggling in our mind against an opposition of forces. Of course, when we are in this struggle, we may have neglected our helmet of salvation that protects our mind against wrong thoughts. Furthermore, we have neglected to have our loins girt with the truth that would have reminded us that God does things in His time not ours (Galatians 4:4), that He is not a man that He can lie (Numbers 23:19), and that whatever He promises, He is able also to perform (Romans 4:21). If we had the breastplate of righteousness on, we would have prevented the wrong thinking from entering into our heart. Once it enters into our heart, it is set up as the idol that will become a stumblingblock to our running the race.

It is imperative that God's soldiers remember that all of His promises have a time factor. We will receive the promise, then comes the testing, the trial of our faith, the storm, or the obstacle of faith. This was revealed in my first book about Storms. It is after the seed of the promise that we had better make sure that we are clothed in the full armor of God. Make no mistake, after the promise, the enemy will attack with his arsenal to get us to doubt God's promise. After all, if he can get us to doubt, we won't get the promise (Hebrews 11:6).

Let's understand that stumblingblocks are not only created by the idols that we may set up in our heart, but they are always in the crowd. The sad truth is that many are in the pulpits preaching wrong doctrines. For instance, they preach the gospel of prosperity where many have gone shipwreck seeking after riches instead of seeking the Kingdom of God first and His righteousness. God's soldiers set up the idol of riches in our heart that became a stumblingblock when it did not take place. If we don't get rid of the stumblingblock, we are heading for shipwreck.

How many have so elevated ourselves that we believe that because we accepted Jesus as Savior that we can live however we want. There's no difference in our life than that of the world. We have become hearers only of the word and not doers. The deception causes us to live in sin. When God's word says that if we do it, we will not inherit the Kingdom of God. God is not a respecter of persons. Evil will be judged as evil even if we believe that we are God's child (Romans 2:11–13). Evil is anything contrary to what God considers holiness, righteousness, etc. We are so deceived that we shrug it off as the loss of some reward.

I have some laugh and say that we may lose a crown or a reward, but at least we'll be there. It must grieve the Lord who has made clear that it is not a reward that will be lost, but Heaven that will be missed. Some have used 1 Corinthians 6:11 and claimed that because we are washed, sanctified, and justified, we are no longer sinners.

That Scripture denotes that because we have repented (turned from our sin), we have been justified by the Holy Spirit. It signifies that we are no longer guilty. We cannot remain in the sin and believe that we are no longer guilty of that sin. That kind of deception is utterly ludicrous to say the least. What we have done is set up that sin as an idol in our heart and allowed it to become a stumblingblock. That is how deceived many are and have believed the lies of the devil over the truth of God's word. In other words, if we don't repent, shipwreck is on the horizon.

This book is essential to all of God's soldiers who are aware of the spiritual shipwreck on the horizon and are determined to avoid it. Only as we become aware of the necessity of contending for our faith will we recognize a possible idol that could be set up in our heart. As we identify this potential stumblingblock, we will contend for the faith, take God's way of escape through His word, and steer clear from it!

9

Giants

And they went and came to Moses, and to Aaron, and to all the congregation of the children of Israel, unto the wilderness of Paran, to Kadesh; and brought back word unto them, and unto all the congregation, and shewed them the fruit of the land. And they told him, and said, We came unto the land whither thou sentest us, and surely it floweth with milk and honey; and this is the fruit of it. Nevertheless the people be strong that dwell in the land, and the cities are walled, and very great: and moreover we saw the children of Anak there. The Amalekites dwell in the land of the south: and the Hittites, and Jebusites, and the Amorites, dwell in the mountains: and the Canaanites dwell by the sea, and by the coast of Jordan. And Caleb stilled the people before Moses, and said, Let us go up at once, and possess it; for we are well able to overcome it. But the men that went up with him said, We be not able to go up against the people; for they are stronger than we. And they brought up an evil report of the land which they had searched unto the children of Israel, saying, The land, through which we have gone to search it, is a land that eateth up the inhabitants thereof; and all the people that we saw in it are men of a great stature. And there we saw giants, the sons of Anak, which come of the giants: and we were in our own sight as grasshoppers, and so we were in their sight (Numbers 13:26–33).

THIS CHAPTER IS MEANT to reveal that Christians must learn to ignore the evil report of the crowd. We may all sit in the same congregation, but that does not necessarily mean that all are led by the Holy Spirit. It is my firm belief that to avoid shipwreck, we must beware of the evil reports from those who lack faith in God and in His ability. Listening to an evil report will cause us to fear the giants and place us outside of the will of God as it did to Israel.

The Scriptures in Numbers narrate the return of the twelve spies that Moses sent out. It's important to remember that these spies experienced the miraculous deliverance from Egyptian bondage, the phenomenal crossing of the Red Sea on dry land, etc.

> And Moses said unto the people, Fear ye not, stand still, and see the salvation of the Lord, which he will shew to you to day: for the Egyptians whom ye have seen to day, ye shall see them again no more forever. The Lord shall fight for you, and ye shall hold your peace (Exodus 14:13–14).

This is the same people that the Lord had made the above promise to at the Red Sea. God told them that He would fight for them, yet when they came back from spying out the Promise Land, ten unfaithful spies caused the whole congregation to disobey God. I am not going to discuss the narratives of Israel's sojourn and their disobedience. The main point for this chapter is that because of their unbelief, they did not enjoy God's promises.

After crossing the Red Sea, they sang, "The Lord is my strength and song, and he is become my salvation, he is my God (Exodus 15:2). Yet, from that point on, they constantly murmured or complained about something. They were hungry, they were thirsty, they were brought into the wilderness to die, etc. The point is that they forgot that God delivered them each time. Bitter water was made sweet, manna was given daily, etc.

Before we were born again, we were in bondage and Satan was our master. And he's a severe taskmaster. Satan always takes and never gives. His goal is to destroy God's ultimate creation which is mankind. Thus, he is always, stealing, killing, and destroying (John 10:10).

Man is the only creation created in His image and likeness (Genesis 1:26–27). Satan hates us because God loves man so much that He gave His life for us (John 3:16). The devil works overtime to get us to do the opposite of what God wills.

1. Satan doesn't want us worshiping God, he wants us worshiping him.
2. Satan doesn't want us believing God's promises, he wants us believing his lies.
3. Satan doesn't want us enjoying God's freedom, he wants us kept in bondage.
4. Satan doesn't want us living in God's blessings, he wants us living in need.

The devil's greatest tool to keep us from God's promises is to keep us in bondage to sin. It can be fear, doubt, unbelief, stress, immorality, etc. As long as he can keep us in bondage, we don't taste the abundant life promised by Jesus. We miss the life that flows with milk and honey. God wants us to see that He desires us to live our life in the fulness of His promises. That's why Satan sends his evil report to cause us to become discouraged and lose faith in God's promises.

At this point, let's get back to the spies. We know that ten gave an evil report and two gave a faith report. Before we look at the two reports, let me interject a little Biblical numerology. The number ten reveals trial or testing, whereas, the number two is a witness or testimony. One report is a lie (evil report), and the other is the truth (faith report). It was a test to see whose report the people would believe. If we look at it logically, there's more evidence in favor of the lie. But faith doesn't go by what it sees, it goes by what it believes (Hebrews 11:1). It is the difference between believing God and not the evil report.

We see that the returning spies claimed that the land surely flows with milk and honey. They brought back pomegranates and figs, plus, the cluster of grapes was so huge that two men had to carry it between them on a staff (Numbers 13:23). The substance of the fruit of the land should have spoken volumes to this people of the blessings that God wanted them to enjoy.

> And Joshua the son of Nun, and Caleb the son of Jephunneh, which were of them that searched the land, rent their clothes: and they spake unto all the company of the children of Israel, saying, The land, which we passed through to search it, is an exceeding good land. If the Lord delight in us, then he will bring us into this land, and give it us; a land which floweth with milk and honey. Only rebel not ye against the Lord, neither fear ye the people of the land; for they are bread for us: their defence is departed from them, and the Lord is with us: fear them not (Numbers 14:6–9).

Joshua and Caleb were really saying, "What shall we then say to these things? If God be for us, who can be against us?" (Romans 8:31). What we have to see from the two reports is that they invoke a question as to which report we will believe. Will we believe the ten who give an evil report that discourages us from doing what God has told us to do? Will we believe the two who give a faith report that encourages us to do what God has told us to do?

When faced with the test, will our flesh give way to fear, doubt, or the hardship it may entail? We can say as we look at this test of Israel that we would believe the two that give the faith report. However, in reality how many times have we listened to the wrong voices in our life and didn't do what we knew that we should have done?

I will interject a story here that is apropos. When my husband was going to marry me, his family (who believed he was crazy to even think of marrying a woman with three children) tried desperately to tell him that he was making a grave mistake. If he had listened to the evil report and not heeded the prompting of the Holy Spirit, he would have disobeyed God. Now, thirty-six years later, we have overcome many storms and experienced the blessings of obedience.

Many in the Church are not living in God's promises, His promise land. We seem to be in the wilderness. We're just getting by, some are lacking, and some are in bondage. I believe the example of the Israelites is how we can learn to enter into His promises.

To understand, we must ask why did they have unbelief? Why did they fear? Why did they doubt God? They had unbelief because they believed the evil report. They feared the giants more than they trusted God. They refused to hear the faith report which should have quickened them to what God had already done. If they had remembered the plagues of Egypt and their protection from them, their Egyptian bondage and deliverance, and their crossing the Red Sea on dry land, they would have hearkened to the faith report.

Anytime we allow unbelief, fear, doubt, etc. to become giants in our life, we will believe the evil report. Faith looks at the magnitude of the greatness of God and believes the faith report. When we see God as He is, those giants seem as grasshoppers.

It's time for God's soldiers to stand by faith in Him against the giants that are keeping us back from enjoying the promises of God. We must understand that although God loves us unconditionally, His promises are not unconditional. It seems that God's promises have "If" clauses. We don't need to list all of them, however Isaiah 1:19 says, "IF ye be willing and obedient, ye shall eat the good of the land."

That makes clear that we may eat the good of the land, only "if" we are willing and obedient. God expects us to obey His commands, and He promises to bless our obedience. Our obedience does not earn the blessings, but it is God keeping His promise. If we think that we deserve or have earned God's blessings, we have forgotten that we are unprofitable servants and have done that which was our duty to do (Luke 17:10).

Let's make something clear here to clarify that the trial of faith that some of us are going through is not because of sin, doubt, fear, unbelief, etc. We are in these hot trials to perfect our faith (1

Peter 1:6–7). It is during these tests that our faith is given a workout to see if we are going to believe God or the evil report. If we truly desire to please God, we will know if we are in sin and refuse to repent. We will know if there's something in our life that doesn't give glory to God and He wants it removed.

If we are to avoid shipwreck in our faith walk, we must identify the giants that are hindering our journey of faith. Is it sin, sickness, or disease? Is it love for the things of this world more than love for God? Are we in constant fear? Do we continuously worry? Is it continual complaining and murmuring about things? Are we always worrying about finances? Is it compromising God's word?

What is the giant that is keeping us from enjoying God's promises? We are not to look at the size of the giant but look to Him who supersedes any giant. There is no bondage that He cannot break (psalm 107:14). There is no sickness or disease that He cannot heal (Exodus 15:26). There is no promise that He is not able to perform (Romans 4:21).

Those of us who are in the fiery trials and not in sin have been given a promise and now our faith is being sorely tested. It's the same question, "Whose report will we believe?" Yes, the trial has been long and arduous. However, we must realize that there is not a time frame between the promise and its fulfilment. Look at Abraham. He waited for twenty-five years for Isaac. How about Joseph who received God's promise at seventeen. He was about thirty-nine when his brothers came to Egypt and bowed down to him. Depending upon the promise, it can take years. It is us who must remain steadfast in our faith during the season of storms that takes place from the time of the promise until its fulfillment.

Have we found ourselves wavering at the promise God has given us? Have we become weary? Have we allowed the wait to cause us to be in sin of worry, fear, unbelief, etc.? Well, it's the same question of whose report we will believe. The evil (lie) report tells us that the giant is too big. The faith report tells us that with God all things are possible (Matthew 19:26).

If we become weary and lose faith in Him, we will wander in the wilderness void of God's promise until we are shipwrecked.

As we step out in faith and believe God's report, the storm may still rage around us, but we will be at peace in Him (Philippians 4:6-7). Then when the fullness of His time has come, the giant will crumble under our feet. God's soldiers are promised that with God nothing shall be impossible (Luke 1:37). Once we take that first step by faith and give no place to the deceitfulness of sin, there is no giant that cannot be destroyed!

10

Temperance

> He that hath no rule over his own spirit is like a city that is broken down, and without walls (Proverbs 25:28).

To HAVE NO RULE over self is to lack temperance or self-control. Without self-control, we will not be enabled to overcome the temptations of this life that could cause us to fall into sin. Jesus knew this and that's why He urged us to deny self and take up our cross daily if we are to follow Him.

> And he said to them all, If any man will come after me, let him deny himself, and take up his cross daily, and follow me (Luke 9:23).

The Lord is encouraging us that if we are going to endure and overcome the difficulties and trials in this life, we must deny our flesh its appetites. If self means more to us than God, we will never deny what it wants. If we are to deny self, we must die out to the self-life, fleshly desire, pride, etc. Without the willingness to have fellowship with His sufferings, God's soldiers will not die to self (Philippians 3:10).

I have always taught that the only way to deny ourselves is to "NOT COUNT." What that means is that if all that matters is Jesus and His will, self doesn't count. That way there is no "ME" in the equation, just God. However, that takes us continuously working to keep our flesh under through temperance or self-control.

What we have to comprehend is that Satan is the enemy of God and our enemy. We must always be aware that he is the schemer always seeking ways to trip us up. In Genesis 4:7, God told Cain that sin lieth at the door. This reveals that he waits for that weak moment to take control over us. Cain's fiercest foe was not Satan or sin lying at the door. It was Cain himself, as it is with us. We have been given the free-will to choose what we do. The choice of obedience or disobedience to God is always ours.

God's soldiers have power or authority over all the power of the enemy (Luke 10:19). Satan cannot make us do anything that we don't yield to his power to do. We have the authority over sin. It no longer has dominion over us. Temperance is a fruit of the Spirit (Galatians 5:23). That means the more we allow the Holy Spirit to be in control of our life, the more self-control that we will have.

Self-control is the power of controlling our behavior, emotions, etc. In other words, we have been given the power to control our thoughts, reactions, actions, what we say, and what we do. But if we choose not to deny self, we will have no control over our flesh. What we have done, in fact, is give the power over to the devil like Adam and Eve did in the Garden.

> But be ye doers of the word, and not hearers only, deceiving your own selves (James 1:22).

Jesus stripped the devil of his power over us and we allow him to control us as puppets with sin. If the devil can convince us that this sin isn't as bad as that, or thinking that we deserve this, we earned it, etc., he can snare us through deception thereby deceiving ourselves. Once we become hearers only and not doers, we are treading on dangerous ground. It is like quick sand and we will be swallowed up by it.

If we are to stand and not be trapped by the devil's lies, we need to be aware of Satan's strategies and tactical maneuvers. As we become knowledgeable of his deceitful ways, we stay clothed in the armor of God and overcome him. What we need to see is that if we give no place to the devil in our flesh, there will be no resurrection of our old man that has been crucified with Christ. Because our body of sin has been destroyed, we should no longer serve sin (Romans 6:6). In other words, if self is dead, the enemy cannot get a foothold in our life. The devil knows that self is our worst foe and is the ends by which he can cause us to become spiritually shipwrecked.

Why is it imperative that we have temperance or self-control in which to deny self? It is quite simple, for it is the only way to dispel the enemy. When the devil tried to tempt Jesus, He denied himself and used the sword of the Spirit which is the word of God each time and gave the devil no foothold. (Matthew 4:1–11). When we do likewise, we give the devil no place to tempt our flesh. What God's soldiers must always remember is that in order to be tempted, we must be drawn away by our own lusts and enticed (James 1:14).

> Lest Satan should get an advantage of us: for we are not ignorant of his devices (2 Corinthians 2:11).

To be ignorant is to lack knowledge, information, or awareness about a particular thing. If we are proficient in the Scriptures, we are well informed about the devil and his deceitful ways to ensnare us. That's why we must be diligent in reading and studying our Bible. We must get the word in us and be skillful with the full armor of God. Then when Satan comes and self wants to listen, we, through the Holy Spirit will contend for the faith, stand fully armed in His armor, wield our sword, and send the devil packing. James 4:7 makes clear that as we submit ourselves to God, resist the devil, he will flee from us!

II

Sentinel

> Son of man, speak to the children of thy people, and say unto them, When I bring the sword upon a land, if the people of the land take a man of their coasts, and set him for their watchman: If when he seeth the sword come upon the land, he blow the trumpet, and warn the people; Then whosoever heareth the sound of the trumpet, and taketh not warning; if the sword come, and take him away, his blood shall be upon his own head. He heard the sound of the trumpet, and took not warning; his blood shall be upon him. But he that taketh warning shall deliver his soul. So thou, O son of man, I have set thee a watchman unto the house of Israel; therefore thou shalt hear the word at my mouth, and warn them from me (Ezekiel 33:2-5,7).

WHAT EXACTLY IS A sentinel? We are God's soldiers that stand and watch. If we are in the army of the Lord, we are all called to be watchmen or sentinels. We are stationed as guards to challenge all comers and prevent a surprise attack. God's sentinels are His watchmen who are to hear the word of God and warn Christians of the danger of spiritual shipwreck. We are to watch over our brethren. If we see them heading for danger, we must warn them.

Spiritual Shipwreck on the Horizon

Because God had set Ezekiel up as a watchman for His people, he was the voice of Jehovah to the whole house of Israel. That meant that he was the voice of God to all God's people to ever remind them of their sins that had been the cause of the captivity, to perfect that which was lacking in their faith, and to remind them of their future blessings.

Let's consider what that is saying to God's soldiers today. It declares that we who know the peril of sin are called by God to be sentinels and warn the ignorant and careless of spiritual shipwreck. We must understand that there is sin and wickedness in the Church. It is in those professing to be Christians. If we doubt that, we need to remind ourselves of Judas who was numbered with the Apostles and had obtained part of their ministry (Acts 1:16-17).

In these last days, we need discernment to recognize what kind of tree we are dealing with. Judas creeps in unawares, turns the grace of God into lasciviousness, and in his life denies our Lord Jesus Christ (Jude 4). It is imperative that God's sentinels start proclaiming the deceitfulness of sin that will lead to spiritual shipwreck. God will not hold us guiltless if we fail to give warning (Ezekiel 3:18).

> Praying always with all prayer and supplication in the Spirit, and watching thereunto with all perseverance and supplication for all saints (Ephesians 6:18).

That scripture clarifies that if we are born again, we are all sentinels. Some, of course, have more responsibility due to our call and position in the Body of Christ. However, that does not mean that we who do not have a call to the five-fold ministry can sit back and neglect our duty as a sentinel in God's army. We are all called to pray and to watch with all perseverance for all saints. Sentinels are to be in prayer and watch out for all of God's soldiers as Ezekiel watched out for all of God's people.

However, a sentinel is to be led of the Holy Spirit and not our flesh. Just because we may have differences in opinion and try to condemn is not being a sentinel. The clothes line preaching has discouraged many Christians. Man continuously looks on the outer and God is looking at the heart. Give them Jesus and allow the Holy Ghost to first transform them by the renewing of their mind, and the inner change will transform the outer. Whatever we do is to be out of love not spite, judgment, jealousy, etc. It is a genuine Holy Spirit concern that warns of shipwreck ahead and the need to steer away from the current course.

What does a sentinel do today? We watch to inform God's soldiers of the false prophets or false sentinels who do not warn of the dangers of the deceitfulness of sin. False teachers see the enemy coming and proclaim that all is well (1 Thessalonians 5:3). These are the compromisers or the teachers who minister to those having itching ears (2 Timothy 4:3).

The sentinel sees the sins in the Church and warns of the danger ahead. Unrepented sin will lead us into shipwreck. Now, God's soldiers are going to be judged for sin, but the sentinels will be held responsible if we don't give warning. However, not all of us are faithful to warn others of the coming danger, and we will answer for our disobedience. Too many of us have become compromisers in order to keep the peace. We don't want to upset others because the truth is like salt on an open wound. In doing so, we have become hearers of the word, not doers, and have deceived ourselves.

What I am saying is that as a sentinel, I am to warn God's soldiers of sin whether I am liked or not, whether it is received or not, etc. My concern must be with souls and their eternal habitation. I must love them enough to tell them the truth even if they consider me an enemy for telling them the truth (Galatians 4:16).

God will still judge sin according to His word, but He will hold me responsible if I haven't given a warning. That is the way it is with all Christians. We are to warn our parents, our siblings, our spouse, our children, our friends, etc. of the repercussions of sin. There must be no compromise because we don't want to hurt their feelings. Because we don't want to offend them, we disobey God and push them into Hell.

The word that the sentinel gives is from God. We must understand that the commission of all sentinels is to give the word of the Lord and warn of the coming judgment. Whether the Church listens is not the concern of sentinels. Our concern is to obey God and sound the alarm. If the sentinels do not sound the alarm, we cannot clear ourselves before God.

Teaching the word of God will not always get positive results. Many say, "Let's get an evangelist who can get results." Getting people all hyped up is not the primary importance. Giving the undiluted word of God is the important thing. God is the One that by His Holy Spirit will work on hearts. It is our responsibility to give the word and leave the results up to God.

> And ye shall know the truth, and the truth shall make you free (John 8:32).

God is not looking for us to get results. He is expecting us to give His word that will set free from sin. He expects us to give His warning of the coming shipwreck. He expects God's soldiers to receive a greater knowledge of what He requires. We must understand that sin in our life will destroy us. Thus, as sentinels, we are to warn of a real Hell that awaits all that continue to live in sin whether or not they said the sinner's prayer five, ten, twenty, thirty, etc. years ago.

How can God that sent His Son to die for our sins (John 3:16-17) have pleasure in our going to Hell? To me, the very heart of God is grieved at us remaining in sin and perishing to an eternal Hell. I also believe that the heart of God is sorely grieved at the sentinels that are standing by in the company of the world and giving no warning. The desire to be accepted by others has caused us to be in danger of shipwreck ourselves.

Once we take to heart what a sentinel is, we will be diligent about our duty. As we see the enemy trying to take God's soldiers captive, we will sound the alarm. If the warning is received, the deceitfulness of sin will be comprehended, and spiritual shipwreck will be avoided!

12

Deception

> Let no man deceive you by any means: for that day shall not come, except there come a falling away first, and that man of sin be revealed, the son of perdition. (2 Thessalonians 2:3).

WHAT EXACTLY IS DECEPTION? According to the Merriam-Webster dictionary, deception is the act of causing someone to accept as true or valid what is false or invalid. The Apostle Paul warned that the day of the Lord will not come before a falling away.

The Greek word for "falling away" is like our word apostasy and refers to a departure from truth. It will be such a defection from the truth of Christian doctrine that it will be completely inefficient to salvation. Evil shall be so unrestrained that mankind will revel in the lusts of the flesh, lusts of the eyes, and the pride of life. It will be a diabolical time of accepting fleshly pleasures and denying the God who created them.

> But as the days of Noah were, so shall also the coming of the Son of man be. For as in the days that were before the flood they were eating and drinking, marrying, and giving in marriage, until the day that Noe entered into the ark, And knew not until the flood came, and took

> them all away; so shall also the coming of the Son of man be (Matthew 24:37-39).

What is that Scripture revealing to us? It is unfolding a truth that before Christ returns many are going to be involved with the world and its pleasures. They will be living as if nothing is about to happen. As the flood took the people by surprise, so shall Christ's coming. All those that are not looking for Christ to return will be as the five unwise virgins revealed in my first book, *Storms Are Faith's Workout*. Being unprepared will find those before the coming of Christ like the unwise virgins who had no oil for the midnight hour. Darkness is when the oil is most needed, for it is in the dark time of storms that we need the light.

If we are thinking that we can partake of the sins of this world and enjoy the blessings of Christ, we are grossly mistaken. That is having one foot in Christianity and the other foot in the things of this world. How many of God's soldiers have allowed themselves to think that they can be a partaker of Christ and a partaker of the world's sins simultaneously? We must decide to be either hot or cold, for there is no acceptable middle road in Christianity. Christians must either be on the side of Christ or on the side of the world. It is time for God's soldiers to step across the line to either be for Christ or be for the world. Of course, that means that we either choose the world and deny Christ in our life, or we choose Christ and deny sin in our life.

> And God saw that the wickedness of man was great in the earth, and that every imagination of the thoughts of his heart was only evil continually (Genesis 6:5).

During Noah's day, wickedness ruled the majority. When it says that the imaginations of their hearts was only evil, it refers to their purposes, their intentions, their desires, and their cravings. Every purpose and desire was led by immorality. They had forsaken God and had given themselves over to the lusts of the flesh, the lusts of the eyes, and the pride of life. God was no longer in their thoughts. Self had become their god and they worshipped self in all its depravity.

Deception

That description seems to portray a considerable amount of mankind today. Sexual sins of all sorts are being flaunted and those who denounce its ungodliness are harassed and persecuted. They are accused of hate speech. If evil men could eliminate the Bible, they would. California at the writing of this book is trying to stop all religious books, even the Bible. However, they will not overrule Him who controls all things, for God's word will endure forever (1 Peter 1:25).

> This know also, that in the last days perilous times shall come. For men shall be lovers of their own selves, covetous, boasters, proud, blasphemers, disobedient to parents, unthankful, unholy, Without natural affection, trucebreakers, false accusers, incontinent, fierce, despisers of those that are good, Traitors, heady, highminded, lovers of pleasures more than lovers of God; Having a form of godliness, but denying the power thereof; from such turn away (2 Timothy 3:1–5).

Perilous means dangerous, treacherous, unsafe, etc. I believe that this perilous time will be for those who are trying to live moral lives. If we look around us, we see the acceleration of corruption. Ungodliness of any type is being accepted and all godliness is being rejected by more and more of society. As mankind becomes haughty lovers of pleasures more than lovers of God, the disintegration of the moral structure of the family and society precipitates.

Lovers of pleasures more than lovers of God in the Greek means that their pleasure is in sensual gratification which has become their god. Today we are experiencing Romans 1:21–32 in a cataclysmic surge with humanity having pleasure in them that do such ungodly deeds. With the speed of ungodliness spreading like wildflowers, Christians are being deceived into compromising the truths of the Bible for the lies of the devil.

What is taking place is what I stated in chapter eight. Christians are ignoring the full armor of God. In doing so, we are permitting the devil's lies to cause us to doubt or compromise God's word. Instead of naming sin as sin, the devil's lies have us going along with the acceptance of sin. What started as a microscopic

Spiritual Shipwreck on the Horizon

leaven is spreading through Christianity and defiling the whole. We are now believing that perhaps God made a mistake in His creation. To accept that people are the opposite of their birth gender is ludicrous.

A male born a male is not a female. A female born a female is not a male. If he was born a female, there would be no need for female hormones. If she was born a male, there would be no need for male hormones. Furthermore, if he was born a female, he would have ovaries and a womb. If she was born a male, she would have testicles. God created us as male or female, He made no mistakes in His creation (Genesis 5:2). It is a diabolical plot of Satan to again cause doubt in God's word as he did in Eve (Genesis 3:1). Those propagating unbelief in God are the advocates for all this chaos of gender. What is truly grievous is that Bible believing Christians have denounced the truth of God's word for the lies of Satan.

The public school system is promoting gender confusion. Satan has infiltrated secular education with his advocates who are causing our young children to be confused about their sexuality. It is a demonic work that Christians are sitting idly by and allowing their children to attend these schools. The lost have no idea of the satanic influence and are deceived by the lies of gender misperception. However, a professing Christian is supposed to know God, His word, and stand against the deceit. Where are God's soldiers? It's time to wake up, comprehend the deceitfulness of sin, and be the voice of God against it. Compromise will lead to shipwreck.

How can this extreme deception take place? The apostle Paul makes it quite clear:

> Now the Spirit speaketh expressly, that in the latter times some shall depart from the faith, giving heed to seducing spirits, and doctrines of devils; speaking lies in hypocrisy; having their conscience seared with a hot iron (1 Timothy 4:1-2).

A departing from the faith means to apostatize or to become shipwrecked. Men will give heed to seducing spirits that will denounce the truths of Christianity. These doctrines of devils will be believed and make the doctrines of Christianity null and void. Deception is the tool of the enemy to cause people to believe whatever is contrary to God's truth. That's why in these last days of men loving themselves more than God, we must be continuously clothed in the whole armor of God and earnestly contend for our faith.

Many will depart from the truth of the Scriptures because our conscience has been seared with a hot iron. Let me explain that. If we have had a severe burn, we lose sensation in that area. In other words, we will no longer be able to feel the prompting of the Holy Spirit. Such deceit is chosen of our own free will. It is giving heed to the seducing spirits that appealed to our fleshly appetites.

Let's understand that not wanting to offend someone is appealing to our carnal appetite that wants to be liked and accepted by all. Not wanting to be called devout, radical, homophobic, etc., is appealing to our carnal appetite to be liked and to be received by all. Most of our compromise of God's word is the desire to be liked by all. Yet, Jesus was hated by the world. If we are not of this world, that is what we should expect (John 15:18-19). A continuance in compromise will lead to our indifference to pleasing God and spiritual shipwreck.

Our protection against deception is to remain completely loyal to God and to be totally dependent upon His word. In these last days, discernment cannot be overemphasized. There will be many flatterers that will seduce many of us who are hungry for man's praise instead of pleasing God. Christians must realize that our old nature is corrupt and will lead us astray. Our flesh and spirit are contrary to one another (Galatians 5:17). The one we feed will be the one that controls. Jesus made clear that to follow Him, we must deny self and take up our cross daily (Luke 9:23). As we deny our self its lusts of the flesh, lusts of the eyes, and the pride of life, our spirit will thrive. Only as we grow spiritually will we be enabled to discern the deception of the seducers or flatterers.

This book is meant to expose the spiritual duplicity of these last days and how to avoid its disaster. Without growing in knowledge and understanding of the Scriptures, we will not have the wherewith to oppose those that try to destroy our faith. As we clothe ourselves in the full armor of God, we will know truth from lies and be enabled to stand against the deceit. Only as we stand against the deception will we comprehend the deceitfulness of sin and avoid the spiritual shipwreck on the horizon!

13

Shipwreck

> For the time will come when they will not endure sound doctrine; but after their own lusts shall they heap to themselves teachers, having itching ears; And they shall turn away their ears from the truth, and shall be turned unto fables (2 Timothy 4:3-4).

To comprehend shipwreck, we must look at apostasy. Apostasy is the refusal to continue to follow or to obey a once held belief. It is an abandonment of a previous loyalty. To apostatize, we must defect or desert from Biblical truths. If we lose heart and become discouraged during storms, when facing obstacles, or fighting physical attacks on our body, we will become weary and give up the good fight of faith. If we apostatize, we are shipwrecked. Contending for our faith will take stamina, will power, resilience, determination, endurance, etc.

Shipwreck is happening today in some who were staunch contenders for the faith. However, the battle has been long and arduous until we gave up hope of overcoming. The weakness of our flesh gave way to the lusts of the flesh, the lusts of the eyes, and the pride of life until we were completely in bondage to the sins that we had been delivered from. Or we quit contending for the faith against false teachers, doctrines of devils, and our old nature.

Such a state does not happen overnight. It begins with seducing spirits like the drip of water that grows and grows day in and day out and it is completely out of hand. Just a drip turns into a puddle. The puddle turns into a pool. A pool becomes a lake. From a lake comes an ocean. If Christians don't nip in the bud the drip, it will continue to grow until it has consumed us with its seductive power.

How can God's soldiers become seduced? Scriptures make clear:

> For men shall be lovers of their own selves
> (2 Timothy 3:2).
>
> Knowing this first, that there shall come in the last days scoffers, walking after their own lusts (2 Peter 3:3).

Today many are teaching that a lack of self-love is why we have so much negative behavior and personality syndromes. When in reality, God's word says that the love of self leads to all manner of evil (2 Timothy 3:2-5). In my book, *Satan's Strategy to Torment Through Physical Ambush*, I exposed Nero, an Emperor of Rome and what his self-love turned him into. Loving self leads to wanting to be worshipped by others. Of course, that is why Satan wanted to exalt his throne above the throne of God. He became puffed up by his beauty (self-love) and wanted to be worshipped by the angels that were worshipping God (Isaiah 14:12-14; Ezekiel 28: 13-18). Pride was the destruction of the devil and pride will be the ruin of self-lovers (Proverbs16:18). Even claiming that we have a low self esteem is really pride because we are not getting the attention we crave.

Self-love causes us to walk after our own lusts which is the true source of infidelity to God. We scoff at the gospel and its bridle of self-control until we are convinced that it is foolishness to live such a life of self-denial. Christians will claim that the Scripture proves that Christ came to give us the abundant life (John 10:10). Restraining our natural appetites is not living an abundant life, for such restraint is harmful to self-expression. Besides God remembers that we are dust (Psalm 103:14). He knows that we are weak, but loves us anyway. The most dangerous of all is we who believe that because we asked Jesus to be Savior that we can continue in adultery, fornication, homosexuality, lying, idolatry, stealing, alcoholism, etc. and go to Heaven (1 Corinthians 6:9-11). If we have truly accepted Christ, we have left such sins behind. We were such, but are washed, are sanctified, and are justified. That means that when we come to Christ, we are no longer partakers of such sins. We no longer walk in darkness, we have done a one-hundred-eighty-degree turn, and have been translated into His marvelous light.

The world is in spiritual darkness and only we have the light to show them the way out of their bondage to sin. Yet, too many of us naming Christ as Savior are living below the grace of God and giving the impression that Jesus is an impotent God.

We are in the world, but we are not to be part of its lusts of the flesh, lusts of the eyes, and pride of life. The word of God is the light or lighthouse to reveal the way out of their darkness. As we live a life that reflects His truths, we are their guides to eternal life. If we are walking in darkness with them, we will partake of their consequences. I know that this is not what a lot of people want to hear. But my books are from the Lord to those who desire to hear, "Well done, thou good and faithful servant . . . enter thou into the joy of thy lord." (Matthew 25:21).

Even some in the Church have claimed that the Bible doesn't condemn homosexual marriage. However the Bible clearly states that marriage is between a man and his wife (Genesis 2:24; Ephesians 5:31). Furthermore, when God claimed that it was not good for man to be alone He created a help meet for him. This help meet was a woman (Genesis 2:18-23). God did not create a husband for Adam, He created a wife. He did not create a wife for Eve, He created a husband. To believe that a man can marry a man, or a woman can marry a woman is to be given over to uncleanness through the lusts of their own hearts and to dishonor their own bodies between themselves. They have changed the truth of God into a lie, and worshipped and served the creature more than the Creator (Romans 1:24-25).

Spiritual Shipwreck on the Horizon

For this cause, God gave them up unto vile affections, for even their women did change the natural use into that which is against nature. Likewise, also the men, leaving the natural use of the woman burned in their lust one toward another. Men with men working that which is unseemly. Because they refused to retain God in their knowledge, God gave them over to a reprobate mind to do those things which are not convenient or proper (Romans 1:26–28).

A reprobate or degenerate mind means that we have stepped over the line from backsliding into apostasy and are completely shipwrecked. God is married to the backslider and will woo us back to Himself (Jeremiah 3:14). If we apostatize, there is no coming back. Our conscience has been seared with a hot iron and is no longer capable of feeling the prompting of the Holy Spirit.

How do God's soldiers start on the road to shipwreck? It starts slowly like a baby learning to walk. We take one step at a time backwards until we are completely backsliding. Let's look at some steps that are revealing that we are on the backslidden road away from God and heading toward shipwreck:

1. Nevertheless I have somewhat against thee, because thou hast left thy first love (Revelation 2:4).
   a. God is not loved first.
   b. Bible reading and study becomes sporadic and then avoidance.
   c. Stop praying regularly and then cease prayer altogether.
   d. Start missing services.
   e. Mind is open to devil's darts.
   f. Listens to seducing spirits.
   g. Believe that God's word is fables, lies, etc.

2. This I say then, Walk in the Spirit, and ye shall not fulfill the lusts of the flesh. For the flesh lusteth against the Spirit, and the Spirit against the flesh: and these are contrary the one

to the other: so that ye cannot do the things that ye would (Galatians 5:16-17).

   a. Resurrection of Old Nature begins.

   b. Gradually start to walk in the Old Nature.

   c. New Nature in Christ begins a slow death.

   d. Old Nature grows in unbelief like Israel in the Wilderness.

3. See 1 Timothy 4:2; Ephesians 4:19; Romans 1:23; 2 Timothy 3:2,4; Hebrews 3:12.

   a. Conscience is no longer sensitive to conviction.

   b. No concern about God's judgment.

   c. Self becomes god.

   d. No longer desire to please God but own pleasures.

   e. New Nature (Faith) has died.

   f. Have departed from God.

   g. At this stage, there is no returning to a life of faith.

> Take heed, brethren, lest there be in any of you an evil heart of unbelief, in departing from the living God. But exhort one another daily, while it is called To day; lest any of you be hardened through the deceitfulness of sin. For we are made partakers of Christ, if we hold the beginning of our confidence steadfast unto the end; while it is said, To day if ye will hear his voice, harden not your hearts, as in the provocation. For some, when they had heard, did provoke: howbeit not all that came out of Egypt by Moses. But with whom was he grieved forty years? Was it not with them that had sinned, whose carcasses fell in the wilderness? And to whom sware he that they should not enter into his rest, but to them that believed not? So we see that they could not enter in because of unbelief (Hebrews 3:12-19).

SPIRITUAL SHIPWRECK ON THE HORIZON

These verses are warning us that an evil heart of unbelief will cause us to depart from the living God. Shipwreck is inevitable if we allow ourselves to harden our hearts against God as Israel did in the Wilderness. We are to exhort each other daily to keep the faith lest any become hardened through the deceitfulness of sin.

Let's understand how we can become hardened through the deceitfulness of sin. It is not intentional rebellion, but the revolt comes about as we look at things logically or realistically. Whenever God is not our first love, we tend to see with our natural eyes, and not with the eyes of faith. A few examples of Scripture will be given to illuminate this truth.

The first is found in Numbers 13:26-14:38 and Deuteronomy 1:19-46 that tells the story of the twelve spies coming back from the Promised Land. They all agreed that it was a good land that the Lord was giving them. But ten spies claimed that the people were strong, the cities were walled, the children of Anak (giants) dwelled there, and that there was no way they were able to go up against such strong people.

Then all the congregation lifted up their voices and cried all night and complained that their brethren had discouraged their hearts.

Moses reminds them that the Lord had promised to fight for them and all that He had done to the Egyptians, but they did not believe the Lord.

It was their decision to listen to the ten spies with the evil report and not the two spies with the faith report. They looked at things through their natural eyes, not the eyes of faith, and disobeyed God that had promised to fight for them.

They were standing at the entrance to the Promised Land and chose to disobey God's command to go in and possess it. That is how they went shipwreck. They allowed their self-preservation to overrule faith in God. Instead of enjoying the land that God had promised, their carcasses fell in the wilderness.

The second is found in Acts 5:1-11 that relates the story of Ananias and his wife Sapphira. They had sold a possession and kept part of the price. Ananias brought the part and laid it at the apostles' feet.

Peter confronted him about lying to the Holy Spirit. While it remained, it was his own. Why did he conceive in his heart to lie to God? Upon hearing these words, Ananias fell down and gave up the ghost.

Three hours later, his wife comes in. When asked if the land sold for so much, she too lied. Then Peter asked her why she agreed with her husband to tempt the Spirit of the Lord. He then informed her that the feet of them that buried her husband were at the door to carry her out.

At those words, she fell down straightway at his feet and yielded up the ghost. The young men came in, found her dead, carried her forth, and buried her by her husband.

Ananias and Sapphira wanted to appear that they were doing like others in giving to the Church, but they wanted to make sure they had some aside for themselves. That was not the sin that led to their death, it was the lying that claimed that they had sold the land for less. This is where they went shipwreck. We cannot lie to the Holy Spirit and not head towards spiritual shipwreck on the horizon.

Peter had told Ananias that the money was his, but his lying was not to man but to God. His lie caused him to go shipwreck. His wife had a chance to tell the truth, and she lied also. Like her husband, she also went shipwreck.

It was their self-love and love of money that caused their shipwreck. They wanted to keep some of the money for themselves. Of course, they didn't have to give any to the Church, but they chose to appear to be pious when they were selfish. Thus, they both died in their sin.

Other examples of spiritual shipwreck in the Bible are Esau who was a self-preserver and sold his birthright (Hebrews 12:16). Lot's wife cared more for the possessions of this life than obeying God (Genesis 19:26). Herod taking the glory that belonged to God (Acts 12:21-23). In Genesis 4:3-8, Cain is jealous of Abel and kills him. Eli's sons were wicked, and he honored or loved them above the Lord (1 Samuel 2:22-36). These are enough to make the point that when God is not our first love, we will go shipwreck.

The book of Jude gives warning against apostasy. Those who are preserved in Jesus Christ are those who continue unshaken in the Christian faith. It also implies that we cannot be preserved in the faith if we do not continue in union with Christ. We cannot have union with sin and union with Jesus at the same time. I am not claiming that we cannot sin once we are saved, I am advocating that we do not have to stay or live in that sin after salvation. As stated earlier, grace gives us power to overcome any sin.

Jude is cautioning us against apostasy or falling away from the faith. Some don't believe that we can fall away, yet how do we become twice dead (Jude 12)? We can explain it away all we want, but twice dead is twice dead. We were dead in our trespasses and sins and become born again. Then we defected from the faith, not backslidden, and died spiritually.

> But I keep under my body, and bring it into subjection: lest that by any means, when I have preached to others, I myself should be a castaway (1 Corinthians 9:27).

In this verse, Paul makes clear that if he did not continue to live a disciplined and holy life, he could become shipwrecked. This is saying that he comprehended that he could fail altogether to get the prize. This was not a reference to the loss of some reward. His flesh must be kept under obedience to the word of God. This could only be accomplished as he exercised self-control and denied himself.

I don't believe that we can lose our salvation. It is the gift of God given by faith in Christ's finished work on the cross. Salvation is our birthright and God will not take away His gift. However, we, as Esau, can sell it for a morsel of meat of fornication, adultery, pornography, drugs, etc. that satisfies our flesh. If we continue in that sin until death, we will die in our unrepentant sin.

> But when the righteous turneth away from his righteousness, and committeth iniquity, and doeth according to all the abominations that the wicked man doeth, shall he live? All his righteousness that he hath done shall not be

mentioned: in his trespass that he hath trespassed, and in his sin that he hath sinned, in them shall he die (Ezekiel 18:24).

We are utterly deceived by the enemy of the cross if we believe that we can never lose our relationship with God. Our sins separate us from Him (Isaiah 59:2). Our salvation is unconditional, but it is not unconditionally secure. There are constant "if" clauses in the word that make this quite clear. We cannot live as we did before and believe that we are going to Heaven, if we do despite the Spirit of grace (Hebrews 10:29). God's soldiers must realize as real soldiers can desert, so can we become shipwreck. If we die in that condition, we will die apart from God.

The wages of sin is death. God's word means what it says. There is no thinking that we can live in licentiousness and go to Heaven. The apostle Paul knew this danger. He was aware of the spiritual shipwreck on the horizon, and he kept his fleshly appetites in check to avoid the deceitfulness of sin. He was aware that at any time, we can sell our birthright for the lusts of the flesh, the lusts of the eyes, and the pride of life. We can experience a right relation with God and then because of our fleshly appetites be carried away from our steadfastness. As Esau, that fleshly appetite will overwhelm us to the point that we gladly sell our birthright to satisfy that fleshly desire.

Yes, Jesus will never leave nor forsake us (Hebrews 13:5), but we can leave and forsake Him. That's why Jude wanted believers to guard themselves against false teachers who were preaching dangerous tenets or false doctrines.

In Jude 4, he reveals that these false teachers had turned the grace of God into lasciviousness which is licentiousness. This is a license for immorality or immoral living. They preached that we could be morally unrestrained and go to heaven.

Let me interject a story about the danger of thinking that you can be saved and live in fornication, adultery, etc. I was talking to a young woman who was living with a man while she was still married to another. When I confronted her, she smiled and said, "Once saved, always saved. I'm saved and Jesus has forgiven me."

I told her the Bible makes clear that she is not to be deceived into thinking that she will inherit the kingdom of God if she lives as an adulterer (1 Corinthians 6:9).

She came back at me with 1 Corinthians 6:11 and said that she is washed, sanctified, and justified by Jesus. I proceeded to tell her that the Scripture in 1 Corinthians talks about what she was before she became saved. The verse explicitly states, "such *were* some of you." That means that you are no longer guilty of what you have repented of. It does not give you license to live immorally and believe that you will inherit the kingdom of God. I Corinthians 6:9 is clear that no adulterer will go to Heaven.

I told her that she is presently an adulterer and unless she repents (no longer lives in adultery), she is going to Hell. In order to be washed, sanctified, and justified, she must no longer live in immorality. Christ did not suffer on that cruel cross to give us license to live in the sins that He died to deliver us from.

> Of how much sorer punishment, suppose ye, shall he be thought worthy, who hath trodden under foot the Son of God, and hath counted the blood of the covenant, wherewith he was sanctified, an unholy thing, and hath done despite unto the Spirit of grace (Hebrews 10:29)?

To deliberately sin after we have received the knowledge of truth is to trample on Jesus. That means that we have no love, respect, etc. for what Christ did for us on the cross. His death was to deliver us from sin, not to allow its deceitfulness to rule in our life. If we do that, we are rejecting His sacrifice for our sins. Rejection means that we are refusing the only access that we have to God.

The gospel of lasciviousness creeps in unawares. It overtakes its victim until we are no longer holiness unto the Lord, but a stinking savor of sin. False teachers teach that we can be saved and live in sin at the same time. I've even heard that our fleshly body has no bearing on our spiritual body. Then why did Jesus live sinless in His fleshly body if the two have no relevance to each other? Plus, we are told in Romans 6:12 that we are not to let sin reign in our mortal body that we should obey its lusts.

SHIPWRECK

Christians are told to study to show themselves approved unto God so that we may rightly divide the word of truth (2 Timothy 2:15). Too many want to listen to the teachers of itching ears, so that they can justify living in the lusts of the flesh, the lusts of the eyes, and the pride of life. All of which is of the world and not of God (1 John 2:16).

Many start out by faith, but after a while, fleshly appetites try to overcome us. Shipwreck doesn't happen overnight. It is a process of degeneration as we gradually turn from fighting our flesh to live in holiness and start our decline into lasciviousness or immoral behavior. It begins with a little compromise here and some more compromise there. We start to accept this as not too bad, then we accept that as not too sinful, etc. We are now living as a hearer only and not a doer of God's word. If we continue to ignore the Scriptures and remain in our sinful condition, we will allow our conscience to become seared with a hot iron. When this happens, we no longer sense the prompting of the Holy Spirit and have allowed the deceitfulness of sin to overcome us. We have permitted our heart to become hardened by sin's deception as did Israel.

That's why Jude exhorts that we must earnestly contend for the faith. This means to struggle to the point that our flesh is agonizing from the conflict between our flesh and the Spirit. When we quit contending for the faith, our old man that was crucified with Christ so that we should not serve sin (Romans 6:6) is allowed to come back to life in all its carnal appetites. How can we once again indulge in sin as a way of life, not a backslider who feels guilty about our sin and will repent, unless our old man has been resurrected? If our old man is completely back from its crucified state, we no longer yearn for the presence of God, are content in sin, and feel no guilt, no shame, etc. about sin, we have gone shipwreck.

I pray that all who read this book will receive the revelation of the possibility of spiritual shipwreck or apostasy of believers, accept its reality, and turn from sin. There is no excuse for us to continue in sin when Jesus has set us free. God's soldiers must realize that if we are living in any of the sins that will not inherit the kingdom of God, we must repent of the sin and the sin of presumption that we can live in sin and go to Heaven. False preachers and teachers will encourage us to live in licentiousness because they are of Satan. The devil knows that all who walk in the flesh will not deny themselves any self-indulgence. In doing so, they will not inherit the Kingdom of God any more than he will.

In my first book, *Storms Are Faith's Workout: Preparing Christians for Spiritual Ambush*, I explained about the importance of loving God with our all and believing in His love for us. Only as we grasp hold of God's love can we overcome the storms of life. If we don't have storms, trials, obstacles, and strategies from the devil, our faith cannot be strengthened. As a body builder will not grow stronger unless there is an increase in the weights, our faith will not become toughened unless it is challenged. Only as we love God with all our heart, with all our soul, with all our mind, and with all our strength, will we trust Him to get us through each storm.

The trial of our faith is not meant to discourage us but to teach us obedience to God's word. Jesus became the author of eternal salvation unto all them that *obey* Him, because He learned through human experience to obey God when confronted with severe anguish in His flesh (Hebrews 5:8-9). Likewise, it is through the sufferings in our flesh that we learn obedience to God's word which strengthens our faith. Earnestly contending for the faith (denying our old nature any ground) will enable us to comprehend the deceitfulness of sin and avoid shipwreck.

My prayer for those who have persevered to read to the end of this book is that they have been enlightened to the deceitfulness of sin, have been enlightened to the truth that compromise has accepted sins that will cause many to miss Heaven, and have been enlightened to the need for boldness to stand against the devil's deception.

If the love of God is truly burning inside us, we will not hold back the truth of sin. Our love of souls will boldly proclaim sin as sin. Knowing that whatever we go through in this life is but for a moment will encourage us to be God's sentinel in this world. Our reward is worth any inconvenience, pain, rejection, etc. that we may have to experience.

However, I realize that those who enjoy their sin will ignore this warning and, in the end, be spiritually shipwrecked. Others who desire with their whole heart to hear, "Well done, thou good and faithful servant . . . enter thou into the joy of thy lord" (Matthew 25:21), will comprehend the deceitfulness of sin, proclaim sin as sin, contend for the faith, and help others to avoid spiritual shipwreck!

www.ingramcontent.com/pod-product-compliance
Lightning Source LLC
Chambersburg PA
CBHW070322100426
42743CB00011B/2518